Arek Hersh ...

A DETAIL
OF
HISTORY

A DETAIL
OF
HISTORY

AREK HERSH

in association with

THE
HOLOCAUST
CENTRE

A DETAIL OF HISTORY
by Arek Hersh

Published in Great Britain by
Quill Press in association with The Holocaust Centre
The Hub
Haskell House
152 West End Lane
London
NW6 1SD

© 2001 Arek Hersh
First Published by Beth Shalom, April, 1998
Reprinted April 1999
Republished by Quill Press, April 2001
Reprinted January 2006, November 2007

British Library Catalogue in Publication Data
A catalogue record for this book is available from the British
Library

ISBN 0-9536280-5-1
(First published with ISBN 1-900381-06-0)

Design and artwork, The Holocaust Centre
Printed and bound by MPG Books Ltd, Cornwall.

Cover Photograph: More than 50 years on, the author stands in the barracks at Auschwitz, describing to students his experiences there.

CONTENTS

INTRODUCTION

It was the end of a long day. The sun was setting in the evening sky, its warmth making the red brick bell tower glow orange. It was undoubtedly a beautiful little church, its neatly trimmed lawns and pansy beds kept meticulously by the nuns from the adjoining convent. The old chestnut tree, broad and tall, had seen the faithful pass by to pray, day in and day out for many, many decades. And Christ hung from his cross above the doorway looking down on us as we peered through the locked gates. Christ and the chestnut tree had seen other things too.

Arek Hersh was only thirteen years old when he was brought to the little Polish Catholic church in Sieradz. Along with his mother, older sister and brother, aunties, uncles, cousins and members of the Jewish community, he was herded in amongst the pews to await his fate. Arek decided to leave the building to beg for water for his family. As he entered the courtyard, he was ordered to join a group selected to work elsewhere. From the moment he stepped out of the church, he never saw his family again. The next day they and all one thousand, four hundred Jews locked into the church were filed out of its doors, deported to Chelmno and murdered.

Arek's story of survival combines the intensely tragic events of a family totally destroyed by the Nazis' policy of mass murder and the intimate details of a community and of people needlessly wasted by these events. If the events he described were a mere detail of history to the Nazis, to the Jewish community and to all who care to stop and think, this remains one of the most challenging moments in the history of the world. Arek Hersh, in his understated and clearly written narrative, spells out just how tragic this was. From his description of life in his hometown Sieradz, to his long journey through the ghettos and camps, this little boy becomes a man who should never have grown up so quickly.

And yet as just a little boy, he makes decisions which save his life over and again. For those who look for survival in armed resistance, take a second look at this little boy and how at times, yes, fate was on his side; but also how often he instinctively manipulated the circumstance to his own advantage. In the end, as fate, chance and pure determination would have it, Arek survived. His family, his community and his civilisation did not.

Our little group huddled together outside the church in Sieradz, listening intently as Arek told his story, locked out of the gates that once locked him in. And the sun went down, the night was cold and the church was grey once more.

Dr. Stephen D. Smith

In memory
of my mother Bluma and father Szmuel,
sisters Mania, Itka and brother Tovia,
and my little Dvora.

Deprived of life.

Dedicated to
my wife Jean,
my daughters Susie, Karen and Michelle.

The new generation.

The market square in Sieradz today. At the age of ten, I was living here with my family, oblivious to the troubles that would soon devastate my carefree world.

GLIMPSES OF CHILDHOOD
Memories of a normal world

Sieradz was an army garrison town with a population of eleven thousand - six thousand Christians and five thousand Jews. The Jewish community was mainly composed of artisans and shopkeepers. It was set in rural surroundings, with forests on its horizons and fields of rape seed shining like gold in the summer sun. It was a peaceful place, the River Warta passing its outskirts, and local history boasting that Queen Jadwiga of Poland had once had a castle here. On the corner of our street, *Ulica Zamkowa* - Castle Street - stood a building with underground passages which led to the castle.

Few strangers came to Sieradz except on market days, when peasants in national costume clattered through the cobbled streets in their clogs. They came regularly to sell livestock, butter, eggs and fruit. When columns of soldiers carrying guns passed by on their way to manoeuvres, my friends and I used to march behind the columns, carrying pieces of wood on our shoulders in place of guns. We used to watch, in admiration, the ceremony of swearing allegiance to Poland, held in the market square with lines of infantry and cavalry all lined up in uniform.

I was born in 1928, the fourth in a family of five children. The eldest was my sister Mania, a dynamic, intelligent and ambitious girl, who at the age of fifteen went to live in Pabianice with my Uncle Benjamin and Aunt Hela as there were more opportunities there for her than there were in Sieradz. Next came Itka, my other sister, a kind, quiet, studious girl, very like my mother in nature, who enjoyed the performing arts and loved to go hiking in the hills. My brother Tovia, four years older than me, was tall and blond, very Scandinavian-looking, and he was a keen sportsman with a good sense of humour. The only child in our family younger than myself was little Dvora, who tragically died of complications after contracting whooping cough at the age of three.

Dvora did not spend all three years of her short life in Sieradz, but in a town called Konin, where we lived for five years from 1931 to 1936, moving there when I was two. The reason we lived there was to be near my grandmother, Flora Natal, my mother's mother, who lived with my Aunt Salka, her husband and their three children. Flora Natal was a fiercely independent woman in her seventies, who earned her living from breeding, fattening and selling geese. Flora's own mother, my great-grandmother, Mindl, had lived till she was one hundred and seven years old.

Because of Dvora's tragic death, one of my earliest memories is of her funeral. I remember the hearse arriving outside our house in Piaseczna Street, the horses draped in black, the driver sitting in front. I remember my sister's body being put into the hearse, then the funeral cortège proceeding up the road, my parents supporting one another in their grief. My sisters walked either side of my parents, whilst Tovia and myself walked behind. I remember the mourners clearly, the men in their black coats and hats, the women in their fox-fur collars, some with shawls over their heads. I remember, also, two beggars walking beside us, all the time rattling their tins, pleading for money. The funeral procession slowly passed by the park where Dvora and I used to play. It was autumn, so the trees and the ground were covered in golden leaves, the birches swaying to and fro in the breeze. We arrived at the cemetery gates, then passed through them to little Dvora's newly dug grave. The path was narrow, the tombstones on both sides inscribed with Yiddish, Hebrew and Polish. As the Rabbi gave a eulogy prayer, committing Dvora's body to the ground, I stood and wept, broken-hearted.

We were a very close, loving family. I respected my parents greatly. My father, Szmuel Jona, was a knowledgeable, even wise man. We were orthodox Jews, faithfully following all the Jewish laws and traditions. Each week my father took Tovia and I to the synagogue. He was a boot-maker by trade, and was kept busy making officers' boots - so busy sometimes, in fact, that he had to employ two people to help him.

My father and mother were both very modern in outlook. They loved dancing and won several competitions. My father was a great believer in socialist ideals, and was very interested in world politics, history and psychology. Often he used to take me to the theatre to listen to political speakers of every persuasion. However, if he did not agree with them he stood up and told them so. He liked to speak his mind and make his point of view heard.

Though he was kind and had a good sense of humour (a trait inherited by Tovia), he was also a great disciplinarian. I remember once he caught me playing cards with some friends, and he took me home and lectured me on the evils of gambling. He never had to resort to violence to make us obey his word, but nevertheless obey we did, both out of respect for his viewpoint and out of fear of his disapproval.

My mother, Bluma (which in Hebrew is 'Shoshana', which means 'Rose'), was a very beautiful and gentle woman. She was slim with high cheekbones and dark hair drawn back into a bun. She put great store in the value of education, and used to tell me that when I grew up she would ensure I received the best possible chance for higher education in order to learn a profession. Her ancestors were Spanish, as could be seen from her looks, and my father's were Russian. My father's family had come to Poland from Russia one hundred and fifty years before; my mother's family could be traced back to the time of the Spanish Inquisition in the Fifteenth Century.

I suppose I was quite a mischievous boy. I did all the things small boys like to do, but shouldn't. However, once in a while my mischief managed to help other people. I remember once, when I was five years old, I fell and cut my leg badly whilst chasing another boy. I was rushed to a local Christian doctor called Grzybowski, who had a practice in the market square. Tovia came too, and after treating me the doctor noticed Tovia limping quite badly and asked him what had caused it. Tovia replied that he had been injured whilst playing football and that the injury just seemed to be getting worse. Grzybowski examined Tovia, and then said that with my parents' consent he would like to operate on Tovia's knee free of charge. My parents agreed, and therefore, due to my naughtiness, Tovia was able to walk much more freely again.

I am not a superstitious man, but nevertheless I feel I must relate a strange incident that happened to me when I was six years old. It all started when my sister, Mania, took me to the cinema. Part of the programme that day included newsreels, and it was at a time when a great Polish leader, Marshal Pilsudski, had just died. The newsreels were full of his great leadership and coverage of his funeral. Mania and I, sitting in the front row, had to look up at the screen, and I remember being engrossed in what I was watching. Suddenly, however, there came a shot of the cavalry charging straight at the screen, and of horses' hooves and underbellies as they leaped over what presumably was a cameraman sitting in a ditch. Being so young, I was absolutely terrified; it had seemed as though the horses were charging straight at me. I felt very ill and couldn't stop shaking, and Mania had to take me home where I was immediately put to bed.

My mother called the doctor, who examined me, and, though he admitted he was puzzled as to what was actually wrong with me, prescribed me some medicine. Tovia fetched the medicine from the chemist, which looked and tasted awful and had not the slightest effect on my condition. I lay in bed, crying and shaking with fear, my body racked with sharp pains. I remember my mother trying to comfort me, whispering soothingly in Yiddish, "*Sha my kind*" - "Go to sleep my darling" - and singing a lullaby, "*Shluf mine kinderle, shluf*" - "Sleep my child, sleep." She was very worried about me, but eventually I drifted into sleep.

I awoke later with the sound of wind driving the rain against the windows. My lips were dry and I felt as though I was burning up. I cried out for my mother, who burst into the room together with my grandmother, Flora Natal, and my father. My mother held me to her body and stroked my face gently. She said to Flora, "What can it be? The doctor doesn't know." For a few moments the room was silent, my father running his fingers through his hair, my grandmother staring at me intently. Then suddenly my grandmother announced that she was going to see a medium called Golda to ask if she could help. Without another word, she left the house.

Half an hour later my grandmother returned, accompanied by an old Jewish lady with a long, bony face, a shawl protecting her head against the rain, and piercing eyes which regarded me intently. The lady asked my mother if she could have a pan and either some wax or candles. These items were provided for her, and she placed the wax in the pan, then began to melt it over the fire. As she was doing this, she placed a hand on my head and began to pray. This went on for quite a while, until finally the old lady removed the pan from the fire and displayed its contents for us to see. To our astonishment the wax in the pan had formed into the shape of a horse. By the next morning I was feeling much, much better.

I leave this open to your judgement as to the explanation for this strange occurrence. Personally I believe the medium, Golda, performed some sort of exorcism over me, ridding me of the terrible fear that had taken a hold. Certainly from that point on I began to recuperate very quickly, and it was only a few days later that I was up and about again and playing with my friends.

Though I loved the peace and beauty of Konin and Sieradz, where I spent my childhood, I still liked to go sometimes to the larger industrial towns such as Pabianice and Lodz. My father took me often on the tram, a journey of about an hour, to visit relatives (and later, in Pabianice, my sister, Mania). I remember being fascinated by the hustle and bustle of city life - by people bargaining on the streets, by bagel sellers pushing small carts, by the sheer scale of everything. Many of the buildings in these cities were large and grey and ugly, serving as factories and textile mills, but I was delighted by them. To me, they were a whole new world.

Probably the only building in Konin which rivalled any of these vast constructions was the local power station. I remember once coming back from a visit to Lodz with my father and being full of the wonders of the big city. I met up with my friends and suggested we go into the grounds of the power station to have a look around, a pursuit which was, of course, strictly forbidden. We climbed the fence which surrounded the station, I typically tearing a hole in my trousers, and once over noticed a hole in the ground covered by grating. Fascinated, we moved forward and began to lift the grating, but just at that moment we heard an angry shout and looked up to see the watchman coming towards us.

Panic-stricken, my friends dropped the grating, which trapped my thumb, and fled, leaving me in a terrible predicament. The watchman released me and took me home to my parents, who were horrified both by my behaviour and by the damage to my injured thumb. I had to have my thumb stitched by the doctor, and then my father gave me one of his stern lectures. Needless to say, I never went near that power station again.

When I was six I started school in Konin, and it was on the way to school that my friends and I encountered one of the characters of the town. He was an old man who dressed in a fur hat, a Russian-type kaftan and high boots with his trousers tucked into them. He had a beard and a large handlebar moustache, and he earned his living by selling edible oils. He owned a horse that he blindfolded with a sack, and which would plod round and round, pulling a wheel which ground the sunflower seeds that produced the oil. We used to watch this process, fascinated.

A DETAIL OF HISTORY

The old man used to stop us and talk to us as we passed by his premises. He would ask us to pull his finger, and as we did he would fart. We were absolutely intrigued by this behaviour, but very soon we got used to him and refused to do his bidding. Instead we used to watch other children fall into the trap, and as they did we would fall about with laughter. The old man never seemed to run out of wind and could always oblige.

In 1936, when I was eight, my family returned to my birthplace, Sieradz. There was much more opportunity for my father's business to prosper in Sieradz as he was a boot-maker and Sieradz was an army garrison town. I was forced to make new friends, though this was not difficult as my cousins, Riven Natal and Sala Judkiewicz, who lived in Sieradz, introduced me to many children of my own age.

I started at a new Hebrew school (*'Heder'*) where I learnt the Bible and *Humish* (the Five Books of Moses) and learnt to translate everything from Hebrew into Yiddish.

Our school was situated near the main highway to Lodz, and took me fifteen minutes to walk to from my house. It was a beautiful walk, especially in the summer, cutting through a large park and also along a path with an apple orchard on one side and a pear orchard on the other. There were also strawberry patches, and in the summer, when the strawberries were ripe, we used to pick and eat them.

The school itself was an old building, and round the back there was a pond where I would spend many happy hours watching the frogs leaping in and out of the water. I used to love watching the animals and birds, and often on the way home I would stop in the park to see the antics of the squirrels, or the storks beside the river Warta bringing food for their chicks.

GLIMPSES OF CHILDHOOD

My teacher at the *Heder* was called Godlewicz. He had a small beard and spectacles and walked with a stoop. In our class were about ten boys, and he would make us repeat a sentence over and over until I grew bored and began speaking to the boy sitting next to me. When this happened, Godlewicz would hit me with the ruler the same amount of times as he had told us to repeat the sentence.

Our house in Sieradz was small, but comfortable and warm. The front of it, my father's shop, faced onto the street and so we used to enter the house through the back, as did our neighbours. To do this we entered through a gate into a partly cobbled yard which was surrounded by buildings on all sides. In this yard were the communal toilets, and strutting about were hens and ducks which we used for eggs and meat.

The house itself had two proper bedrooms - one for my parents and one shared by Tovia and I - and another smaller bedroom at the front which my father had converted by reducing the size of his shop, and which my sisters shared. The other rooms included a lounge, a bathroom and a kitchen, and beneath the house a cellar, where vegetables and other perishable goods could be kept cool.

Our furniture was wooden and old-fashioned, and our ornaments were few. I remember the candlesticks that we used to have, and also a large conch shell which we children used to hold up to our ears to listen to the sound of the sea. On the walls in the lounge were photographs in oval frames of our family and grandparents, and on the floor were rugs, but no carpets. Each room possessed a beautiful tiled fireplace as high as a door, which kept the house warm in winter, and in the kitchen was an old iron cooking range with a metal flue which went up through the roof. The proximity of our neighbours, and the strong religious and family bonds, meant that there was always a great sense of community and love in our lives at this time.

Sieradz too had its share of characters. Perhaps the most memorable of these was Mordechai the *Wasertreger*, which means 'water carrier' (within Jewish society people were always known by their trades, such as Itzhak the baker or Moishe the tailor). Mordechai was a very large, heavy man with a small beard, and he used to wear a large jacket with a *tzitzis* - a ritual garment with fringes - hanging from beneath it, trousers tucked into his boots and a skull cap on his head. With a wooden yoke across his shoulders, he looked very comical.

In the winter, which in Poland was bitterly cold, I used to watch Mordechai filling up his buckets from the street pump and delivering the water house to house. As nobody had water laid on in their homes, he performed a valuable service. However, because the spilled water from the pump froze quickly into ice during the winter, the ground around the pump was treacherous, and time and again we saw Mordechai fill up his buckets only to slip and fall, spilling cold water over both himself and the already ice-covered ground. On a number of occasions when this happened, I remember my cousin Riven and myself running up to Mordechai, taking the buckets from his yoke, and filling them for him at the street pump. Then we would help him to his feet so that he could carry on with his work. Each time we performed this service for him, Mordechai would not say a word, but would simply touch our heads in silent and heartfelt thanks. Then he would turn and trudge off into the snow.

But though collecting water from the pump was one of the more unpleasant sides of winter, we children still used to have a great deal of fun when the winter months came along.

GLIMPSES OF CHILDHOOD

When the river froze over, we used to go down and skate on it. Often I used to go home with my head covered in bumps where I had fallen over, which my father would press with a silver coin to reduce the swelling. As well as ice skating I also loved sledging, and had my own sledge which I had made from wood and iron bands which were used to bind packing cases. I used to lie flat on my stomach on my sledge and launch myself down the steep slopes, guiding myself along with the toecaps of my shoes.

We used to watch as horses and carts delivered large chunks of ice that had been cut out of the river Warta. This ice would be sprinkled with sawdust and stacked in a large ice house where it would stay until summer, when it would be used for such things as making ice cream and in hospitals.

Though the winters were severe, they did not prevent the peasants from coming into Sieradz on market days. They would appear on sleighs pulled by horses with bells round their necks. It was a lovely sight. Often we used to hang onto the backs of sleighs and be pulled along until the driver spotted us. Then he would lash out with his whip, and we of course would let go quickly.

Another trick of mine was to tie the rope of my sledge onto the back of a horse-drawn sleigh when the driver was not looking. This way I used to travel many kilometres without the driver being aware of me. On these occasions all that could be seen of the driver would be a small part of his face. It would be so cold that icicles would hang down from his beard and moustache. The drivers would invariably be dressed in sheepskin coats, fur hats, gloves, ear muffs and high boots. In their pockets they would keep small bottles of vodka from which they would take a swig now and then in order to acquire a little inner warmth.

A DETAIL OF HISTORY

In fact it was so cold during these winters that it was a rare occurrence to be able to look out of the windows of our house as the ice would be so thick. Fortunately, however, the houses themselves were lovely and warm inside, for even in those days we had double glazing. Perhaps the best thing about winter was that some days the snow drifts were so high that we could not go to school.

One pursuit that we shouldn't have done at all, particularly in the winter months, was climbing up the partially-built school which was not far from *Ulica Zamkowa* - Castle Street - where I lived. A few of my friends and I would go to the construction site when it was empty and would climb up the half-built structure, jumping from joist to joist, barefoot for a better grip, as we ascended from first to second floor and so on. Looking back now, it makes me shudder to think we used to do this. One slip would have meant instant death, but in those days this type of danger did not occur to us.

However, life was not all play. I had to do my share of errands as well. One errand I particularly disliked was having to fetch the milk from a farm in a village about three kilometres away. This farm was owned by a man named Janek, who had previously worked for my father as a bootmaker, but who had inherited the cattle and poultry farm when his father had died. I used to have to wait until the cows were brought in from the fields and milked before the farmer could fill the metal urn I had brought with me. I also used to buy some of his butter and cheese before returning home. This was a time-consuming errand and one that I wished Tovia and Itka would share with me.

As orthodox Jews, our religion was very important to us. There were certain rituals and festivals that we followed scrupulously. Every Friday before dusk my mother would '*bench licht*' (kindle two candles), which was the signal that the Jewish Sabbath had commenced. Like all good Jewish wives, my mother would ensure that her house was spotlessly clean at this time, with a crisp white tablecloth on the table, the cutlery shining and an extra special meal prepared. As my mother lit the candles, she would bring her hands towards her face several times and would say in Hebrew the prayer, 'Thank the Lord, our God, King of the Universe.'

My father would then take Tovia and I, washed and dressed in our best clothes, to the synagogue. After the service was over we would return home, and upon entering the house would wish my mother and my sister, Itka, 'Good Shabbat' (Good Sabbath). Then we would all stand round the table as my father made *Kiddush* - 'grace' - with a silver cup of kosher wine. He would take the first sip, then pass the cup round for the family to share. Then he would uncover a *halla* - plaited bread - that had been specially baked for the Sabbath. He would say grace again, then cut the bread, put a little salt on it, and give us all a piece to eat.

After this my mother would serve the meal. This would consist of freshwater fish to start, followed by chicken soup with *Kneidlach* - matzo balls - and then a main course of chicken or duck with roast potatoes and vegetables, and a sweet to finish. The meal would be rounded off with a drink of lemon tea, which we sweetened by holding a cube of sugar in our mouths. After the meal we all said grace one more time.

On the Saturday morning my mother and father would take us again to the synagogue. There we would listen to the Cantor, who had the most beautiful voice, singing the prayers to the congregation. One *Yom Kippur* evening the Cantor sang *Kol Nidre*, and it was one of the most moving things I had ever heard. This cherished memory will remain with me for as long as I live.

A DETAIL OF HISTORY

We returned from the synagogue at midday, whereupon I would be sent to the bakers to collect the *Cholent*, a concoction of potatoes, meat, bones, barley, or whatever else one wished to put into it. This would have been taken to the Jewish baker early on Friday afternoon before the Sabbath; for a small payment, he would put the *Cholent* into his oven and cook it very slowly. The *Cholent*, eaten on Saturday, always tasted wonderful.

On Saturday afternoons, if the weather was fine, the entire family - and many other Jewish families - would go to the park, where I would play with my friends or take a stroll with my parents down to the river Warta. All this was to leave a great impression on me - the family life, the sense of belonging, the customs, and the love we had for one another and for our neighbours. It is a much cherished part of my growing up, my heritage and my life.

My favourite of all Jewish festivals was *Purim*, which comes usually around February or March. The story of *Purim* is about the deliverance of the Persian Jews from the hands of a terrible oppressor called Haman. When this festival came around, I would go to the synagogue with my father, holding in one hand a flag covered in different pictures with a red apple stuck on top of it, and in the other hand a *gregger* - wooden rattle - which, when twirled around, made the most dreadful noise. The reader in the synagogue would tell the story of Purim, and each time he mentioned the name 'Haman', everybody, but especially the children, would stamp their feet and twirl their *greggers* and generally make as deafening a noise as possible. This action, repeated many times during the service, must have made the poor reader a nervous wreck, but it was lots of fun for us children.

My second favourite festival was *Pesach* - Passover - which usually comes around April. I remember helping my mother clean out all the *chumetz*, which is everything that contains leaven, in preparation for this. We had to be very thorough. No cupboards or drawers could be left untouched, and even pockets had to be emptied in case they contained crumbs. All the everyday crockery and cutlery was stacked in the cellar, and we would replace it with the special set reserved only for *Pesach*. The pans would be scalded out with hot stones and water, and any *chumetz* found would be burned in the back yard.

The story of *Pesach* is re-enacted every year, and tells of the Israelites being freed from bondage in Egypt. On the first and second evening of *Pesach*, the whole family would sit round the table while the man of the house recited the *seder* - service - then we would all read the *Hagada*, which is an illustrated book describing the exodus of the Israelites from Egypt, their wanderings through the desert for forty years, and finally Moses receiving the Ten Commandments on Mount Sinai. Being the youngest member of the family, I would read the *Mah Nishtana* - Four Questions - from the *Hagada* to my father.

Pesach was an eight-day festival, a family feast during which everybody wore their new clothes. On the dining table would be *Matzo* - unleavened bread - bitter herbs, much wine and many different types of food that my mother had prepared specially. These festivals were happy and unifying events among the Jewish community.

On Tuesdays and Fridays I often used to accompany my mother to the market, and help her bring back the poultry - live ducks, geese or chickens - which she had purchased. These, the peasant farmers had brought in from surrounding farms, as they had also brought butter wrapped in wet leaves to keep it fresh and eggs in wicker baskets. The peasants were mainly ethnic Germans

A DETAIL OF HISTORY

and were very picturesque and colourful in their Polish national costumes. I used to listen to my mother bargaining with them.

We would also buy fish - mainly freshwater fish such as carp and pike - from the fish market in front of my Uncle Pesach's butcher's shop. (Uncle Pesach was my mother's brother.) Like the poultry, the fish were very fresh; I used to watch them swimming around in large metal barrels.

When we arrived home, my mother would send me to the *Shochet* with the poultry. He was the man who killed poultry and cattle according to the Jewish tradition. His workplace was a wooden hut behind a small synagogue and next to the *Mikvah*. This building housed separate public baths for men and women. Bathing in the *Mikvah* was a regular weekly ritual for Jewish women, and was a place they were required to go before getting married. Also every Friday evening, before the Sabbath, the men would go and bathe there too. I remember going along with my father several times when I was a young boy.

One companion from my boyhood, whom I have not yet mentioned, was Zlata. She was my dog, a shaggy and not very beautiful brown and white mongrel, who was given to my parents by a farmer when she was two months old. Zlata and I loved one another at first sight, and as she began to grow out of her puppy stage, I took her everywhere I went. We would go for a run in the fields or down to the river to fish. I remember her cocking her head to one side and pricking up her ears as I talked to her. She was a very intelligent dog and we became inseparable friends.

One way in which she helped me was when I contracted German measles. At that time I felt so ill that I didn't want to eat any cooked food. When the meals were served up, therefore, I would ensure Zlata was under the table, covered by the long tablecloth, and I would secretly give her all my food. This solution pleased everybody - Zlata, myself, and my parents who thought my appetite had returned.

A year passed, and our friendship was such that Zlata never bothered with any other member of the family except me. One morning I saw my friend, Heniek, running towards me. He was very agitated and told me that the *Hycel* - dogcatcher - had taken Zlata away. We both ran to the market square just in time to see the *Hycel* moving away with his daily catch, and Zlata imprisoned in a cage. When she saw me she started whimpering. I was shocked and heartbroken; the tears poured from my eyes.

I ran home as fast as my legs would carry me and poured out my story to my father, who hired a passing *droshke* - hansom cab. We then travelled as quickly as we could to the *Hycel's* quarters, which was on the outskirts of town. My father explained the situation and paid him some money, and thankfully the *Hycel* released Zlata back to me.

Several months later, Zlata had a litter of puppies - two black ones, one brown one, and one that was the image of Zlata herself. They were very cute and I used to watch them feeding, but after three months my parents gave them away.

Zlata's sad end came one day when I heard yelping and whimpering in the street outside. I ran out of the house, and saw to my horror that she was lying on her side in the road, having been run over by a passing horse-drawn cart. I hoped that by some miracle she would survive, but she did not, and I cried my eyes out, heartbroken. Tovia fetched a sack and a box, and we took Zlata to a field and buried her. I put a stick in the ground to mark her grave. Every so often I went to visit the grave, and once there would remember Zlata as she was - happy and lively and playing with me once again. To me, she had been a member of the family, and I often cried for her. So ended my friendship with my best pal, little Zlata.

The eleventh year of my life, 1939, began like any other. I was still doing all the mischievous things that boys of my age do - climbing trees either for conkers or walnuts or fruit and being chased by the park keeper. We generally had fun, and occupied ourselves with games such as *Palant*, played with a bat and a piece of wood that was pointed at both ends (the idea being to hit one of the points with the bat. The stick would fly into the air, and the player would hit it again. Whoever hit it furthest would be deemed the winner). We were little aware of the wider world situation, or of the impending crisis that would soon devastate our own.

I think the first indications that all was not well for the Jewish population came in October 1938, when German Jews of Polish descent began to be sent across the border to Poland. As Sieradz was only fifty miles from the border, many of these Jews came to our town, full of stories about the inhumanity of the Nazis and about how badly Jews were being treated in Germany. However, though these people were being forcibly removed from the country and allowed to take only a few possessions with them, they were well-fed and smartly dressed and seemed to be of the general opinion that things in Germany would soon improve and they would be able to return home. A committee was set up in Sieradz to help these people, and they were absorbed into the Jewish community. Though we personally couldn't take anyone as we had no room, my father helped organise homes for all those who were sent across the border to Sieradz.

Another indication of the growing strength of Nazism at this time was the higher degree of antisemitism among the *Volksdeutsche*

- ethnic Germans - living in and around Sieradz. I remember one market day I went into a Jewish-owned shop in the market square, and as I entered, two Christian Poles stopped a couple behind me, a peasant and his wife, with the words, "Don't go into this shop. It is owned by Jews."

Even among the children, antisemitism began to increase. On many occasions we would come out of school to be apprehended by Christian boys shouting, "Dirty Jews, go back to Palestine!" The worst experience I had was when I was sitting on a park bench with a nine-year-old friend of mine. Two Poles in their twenties came up to us, and one said, "Jews are very lucky. If the Germans hadn't come into Poland, we would have slaughtered all of you."

As a child I did not realise the deep meaning behind all these actions, but the blind, senseless hatred I suffered will be ingrained in my mind for as long as I live. I did not understand why we were suddenly being treated as second-class citizens: Jews in Poland did their military service, they fought for their country; my father himself was a case in point. However, it must be stressed that this mindless racism did not extend to everybody. We still had many non-Jewish Polish friends who were really wonderful to us.

In the cinemas the newsreels began to show how Poland was preparing for war. It showed the Navy displaying their battleships and the Air Force flying their planes in formation. To me this meant little as I had never seen war before, and all I knew about it was what my parents had told me about the First World War and about how inflation was so ridiculously high that they had to go out with a suitcase full of money to buy provisions. The general attitude among the Jews at this time, an attitude shared by my parents, was that the Germans were decent people with whom you could do business and surely they couldn't have changed that much.

A DETAIL OF HISTORY

As it turned out, this was a very dangerous attitude to have. To us, the soldiers who were entering Sieradz in ever increasing numbers were not portents of disaster, but simply people to sell lemonade to during the summer. At this time, Tovia and I were members of '*Hashomer Hatzair*,' a Socialist scout group. We were like soldiers ourselves as we marched through the town, some boys playing trumpets, others playing the drums. We wore a uniform of grey shirts, grey shorts and blue cravats, and we were very pioneer-oriented. We went on summer expeditions, led by our group leaders, Nahum Ozorkowicz, Yosef Kutner and Hanna Godlewicz, where we were given a tent between four of us and sent out into the countryside to fend for ourselves. We used to dig up potatoes, make a fire and bake the potatoes under cow dung. This way we learned to be self-sufficient, and to think and act for ourselves, and not to be too dependent on other people.

Looking back, I think this was probably the best training I had in preparation for the terrible war to come.

Ethnic Germans stand over a Polish village as it is
burned to the ground, after the invasion of Poland in
September 1939.

STORM CLOUDS
A foretaste of brutality

Storm clouds were gathering over Poland. My father and his friends
would stand outside the synagogue with their prayer books in their
hands and one would say, "There will be an invasion," while another
would argue that there would not.

My thoughts were full of my family, my friends and the
memory of Zlata. I had no experience of going through a war, but
my father had told me stories about World War One, how people
suffered and how many millions of soldiers had been killed. My
parents frequently listened to the radio for the latest news, and
after each news broadcast they would discuss the situation.

One day, as I was walking towards the market square, I saw
that people had gathered outside a house. As I got nearer I noticed
the window was open and the people were listening to Hitler, who
was ranting and screaming on the radio. I understood much of
what he was saying as Yiddish is very close to German. Sieradz

and the surrounding villages had a great many ethnic Germans, and on Tuesdays and Fridays, which were market days, the peasants brought the poultry, butter and eggs to my mother. She would speak to them in German. In this way I soon picked up much of the language.

One hot day, towards the end of August 1939, I was sitting looking out of the window when I saw a column of soldiers marching past our house followed by three armoured cars and several cannons drawn by horses. They were '*Uhlans*' - Polish cavalry - looking very distinguished in their four-cornered hats trimmed with multicoloured bands, swords at their sides and high black boots with stirrups. Two planes were flying high overhead, and I thought, 'What an invincible army we are. We Poles will stand up to the Germans, we will teach them a lesson and nobody will push us around.'

Having noticed my friend Heniek and my cousin Riven following the soldiers down the hill and along the cobbled street, I decided to join in the marching.

Many of the soldiers were slipping as their boots had nails on the soles which made marching difficult. We reached the bottom of *Ulica Zamkowa* where a wooden bridge had once stood. During the previous year the bridge had been demolished with part of the road by floods. We approached a small village which was on the outskirts of a town. It consisted of four small cottages and a horse and cart.

Eventually, we stopped where Queen Jadwiga once had a castle. All around were open fields; in the distance were forests and the river Warta. The farmers were gathering the harvest and standing the sheaves of wheat up to dry in the hot sunshine. In the distance, fields of yellow rape seed were growing. Everything was so peaceful.

STORM CLOUDS

Suddenly the army column was brought to a halt. An officer galloped towards us and told us to leave as his men were going on manoeuvres. There was nothing else for us to do except go home, but we thought we would return by the route over the river. We saw two kayaks moored at the riverside and it seemed like a good idea for us to have a go. Heniek was a bit of a show-off, and decided to stand up in the boat. However he lost his balance and fell into the river, losing his oars in the process. This would have been funny had it not been for the fact that he was not a very good swimmer.

Riven and I tried to reach out to Heniek, but we just couldn't get to him, so I decided to push the other kayak out and help him. As I came near to him he grabbed the end of my boat and, in his panic, turned me and the boat upside down. Now we were both holding on for dear life. From a distance we could hear shouting and cursing coming from the direction of a tannery which was at the side of the river. As we floated nearer, we recognised the person doing the shouting as Fairvel, the son of the owner of the tannery, whom we all knew. He helped us out of the water, both of us naturally drenched to the skin. I was very fearful of going home in that condition.

I decided it would be a good idea if I walked into the house crying. Maybe, I thought, that would help my situation. Luckily for me my mother was alone in the house, and washed and dried me and gave me some fresh clothes to put on. She also scolded me for going to the river, explaining how deep and dangerous it could be.

By now the storm clouds were truly gathering over Poland. Men were starting to be called up into the army. The new recruits would walk around the town in their new uniforms, tan belts with shoes to match. As Sieradz was a garrison town there were many soldiers around.

A DETAIL OF HISTORY

The prison, which was situated at the end of a park, was very large. It had high walls surrounding it, the tops of which were covered with broken glass. Daily it was filling up with hundreds of Germans suspected of spying, who were brought into Sieradz by the trainload. I watched them being marched into the prison, just like an army going through the prison gates. By this time, everybody was talking about the impending war. One day my father got his 'calling up' papers. He had served in the cavalry in the First World War, and thought that with his previous experience he would be sent to the front line. He was instructed to report to Kutno in two weeks' time, and my mother naturally was very upset at the prospect of my father leaving us. However, despite our feelings, we all knew that he had to go; one cannot run away from one's duty to one's country.

It was now the end of August 1939. One Saturday I remember sitting with my older brother, Tovia, outside our house. We had just got back from the synagogue and everything was calm, when suddenly, from out of nowhere, we heard the sound of a plane. This was immediately followed by a barrage of rifle fire as soldiers began firing at the plane, which swooped low over the houses, then flew away.

The impending situation was now being discussed at great length. I remember hearing my father talking it over with his friends. He said that the Polish army were going to make a stand on the other side of the river Warta, which was very wide at that particular point, and was situated about three kilometres from the town.

The plan was thought to be that the Germans would be allowed to take Sieradz intact with its newly built barracks on this side of the river, whilst the Polish army waited for the Germans on the other side and made a stand.

STORM CLOUDS

The battle lasted for about eighteen hours. Although the Polish army put up a very brave fight, the plan failed. They were quickly defeated by the weight of the German army.

Before this event occurred the population of the town were ordered to leave. My father, who did not have to report for another two weeks, thought we should leave immediately, and that we should go to some relatives who lived about fifteen kilometres away in a town called Zdunska Wola. We all wanted to get across the river and away from the battlefield zone as soon as possible. There was no available transport, as the Polish army had commandeered all motorised vehicles, and even horses and carts were difficult to obtain. So we loaded up with the essentials and whatever else we could carry, then my father locked the doors of our house and we started forth on our journey. Just before we left, however, I asked my father if I could say goodbye to my cousins who lived several houses away from us. There was Sala, Bluma and Genia Judkiewiecz and their parents, and also my uncles Pesach, Moshe, Natal and their families.

I could see the Judkiewieczs coming out of their house and climbing into their own *droshke* - hansom cab - with their few possessions. With them having such a large family to take, there was no room for us. We said our goodbyes and hoped that with God's help we would see each other soon. Then we parted.

We started walking towards the bridge that spanned the river. At this time all was quiet. There was no outward sign of the impending battle. I remember looking down at the river and thinking to myself, 'Everything looks so peaceful.' People were walking with their families to get away from the battle line. Near the river's edge a few soldiers were digging trenches, and several *Uhlan* cavalry were riding on their horses. As we passed out of

A DETAIL OF HISTORY

Sieradz and began walking away, two armoured cars passed us on the road.

A little further along, my father decided to get off the main route and rest in a village. We sat on a grass verge that was near two cottages with thatched roofs. They must have been very old as they were leaning over to one side, their doors so small that whenever the farmer and his wife went either in or out they had to bend down. My father took me with him to one of the cottages, to ask the farmer if we could buy some milk. When we entered, I saw the floor was just uneven earth. The farmer's wife was sitting in a rocking chair. She was wearing the Polish national costume that most peasants wore. She had a white scarf on her head, which emphasised her rosy cheeks. The farmer asked her to get us some bread, and she struggled to get out of her chair, she was so fat.

Soon the farmer came back with a small churn which contained milk and a large loaf of home-made bread. My father wanted to pay for it, but the farmer would not accept any money. He said to my father, "May God watch over you and your family."

We ate, drank and rested a little longer as my mother was tired. We had been walking for three hours with heavy parcels. My brother, Tovia, and my sister, Itka, carried the heaviest parcels as they were much older than myself. We started our journey once again, passing beautiful fields covered with buttercups where cows and horses were grazing.

Eventually we came to a large forest that contained silver birch and fir trees. At this point my father decided to get back onto the main Sieradz-Zdunska Wola road. As we approached this point, we saw people pushing small carts with their belongings piled on, and children hanging on to their mothers' skirts. In fact, it was not just carts being pushed, but anything with wheels that might make transportation during the journey easier for them. Families were carrying bedding and whatever else of their few belongings they could manage. Now and then an army vehicle passed us, going in the direction of Sieradz. We passed several villages and knew we would soon be at our destination.

By three o'clock in the afternoon we could see Zdunska Wola in the distance, and at four-thirty reached Sieradzka Street. Hot and weary, we made our way to our relatives, who were delighted to see us. After some food and drink, we told our relatives what had been happening in Sieradz. While the 'grown-ups' were talking, I ran next door to where my uncle Moshe lived with his two sons, David and Tovia, and their sister Mania, who were very pleased to see me.

Suddenly we heard a noise in the sky. We all ran out into the street to watch a dogfight between German and Polish fighter planes. Fortunately in this fight no one was injured, and after a short while they flew away.

The night passed peacefully, and the next morning I went into the yard that was at the back of my cousin's house. At the end of the yard was a fence and then fields, growing maize. Suddenly there came the deafening roar of engines as several planes started dive-bombing. I looked up and saw the German Cross on the planes' fuselages. There were no Polish planes in sight or any sound of anti-aircraft guns to be heard. The planes started strafing and dropping bombs all around, and then wave after wave of other planes came, filling the sky, their noise deafening. They bombed and strafed everything and everyone in sight, creating panic among the civilian population, as was their objective.

People were running in all directions. I dashed into the maize fields, not realising what I was doing. Soon another wave of German '*shtukas*' came swooping down, the noise so appalling that we couldn't tell which direction they were coming from. Two planes dived towards where I was hiding. When I realised that they were coming towards me, I ran back towards my cousin's house. Apparently my parents were out, frantically looking for me. My brother was calling me, "Arek, where are you?" I called out, "Here!" Suddenly there were more planes coming in our direction, bombing and strafing as before. I ran towards the railway station, not realising that this was the wrong thing to do. As I ran through the maize field taking cover amongst the tall, thick plants, another plane started to dive-bomb towards me. Panic-stricken, I ran towards a road. To my right a horse lay dying, beside which was a man, a woman and three children. They must have been the victims of a direct hit as they were all badly injured, two of them having had their legs blown off in the blast. A terrible fear overcame me. I changed direction, and once again started running towards my cousin's house when suddenly everything went quiet. Their mission apparently over, we watched as the planes turned and flew away.

By now my parents had spotted me from a distance. How happy I was when I saw them again. I thanked God for delivering us from that dreadful nightmare.

As a result of this ordeal, my father decided that it was too dangerous to stay in a town, and that maybe it might be better in a village. We said our goodbyes to our relatives and started on our journey. We made our way towards a large forest, passing fields with fruit trees on both sides of the road. Soon Zdunska Wola faded from our view. Still nervous and fearful from our experiences, we kept our ears open for approaching planes. As we neared the forest we passed a small white building, where we were stopped by two *Kanarki* - military policemen. They asked us where we were going, then asked my father for his papers as he was of military age.

STORM CLOUDS

He handed the papers over, and after reading them they informed him that there was no way he could get to his military base as Poland was at war.

Half an hour later, they let my father go, and we continued walking for another three kilometres. From a distance we saw a small wooden farmhouse, which, as we approached, we could see was surrounded by a fruit orchard. Two Alsatian dogs were barking ferociously at us, though they were fortunately both chained to the side of the house. My father and brother knocked on the door, while my mother, sister and I waited at the gate. A farmer answered, and my father asked him if we could stay the night as it was getting dark. The farmer kindly agreed, but could only offer us his barn as he had four small children and there wasn't room in the house. We accepted gladly. The farmer and his wife were ethnic Germans. They were frightened, not knowing how the Polish people would react to them, wondering if they would become scapegoats for revenge. The farmer's wife in particular was extremely nervous, and kept crossing herself. They were very poor people who had no land, but worked in the forest cutting down trees.

We made our bed on bales of straw, and we were so exhausted that we slept peacefully that night. Next morning, after washing at a water pump, and paying the farmer and thanking him for the food and shelter he had given us, we started our weary way back towards Zdunska Wola. My father had now decided that we should all go to Lodz.

Once again we stayed with our cousins for a couple of hours. My brother took me to see the damage in the town square, where there were several huge craters from the bombing and some dead horses lying about. All around, windows had been blown out and several textile buildings shattered.

A DETAIL OF HISTORY

After lunch we started on our way to Lask, keeping to the country roads as the main ones were packed with civilians and army personnel, all in a panic, aware that any moment German planes could strafe them. We crossed open fields, the sun shining overhead in a blue sky. Some Polish cavalry passed us with horses pulling several artillery guns. A high-ranking Polish officer drove past in a chauffeur-driven car, then came infantry soldiers singing a rude army song. As we approached a railway yard, my father decided we should sit and have a rest under a tree. We sat there, looking at a goods train standing on a line with no engine attached to it.

Suddenly we heard the roar of planes overhead, and quickly ran to a nearby orchard to try and find some cover. As we started to run, the planes appeared and began strafing and bombing the train that was full of ammunition. All hell broke loose as the ammunition exploded, bullets ricocheting in all directions. Everybody in the area began to run for their lives, the Polish units of cavalry and infantry men scattering in all directions as they were pursued by the German fighter planes, creating havoc and panic. I saw two soldiers on horseback who were pulling a gun carrier behind them, when all at once one of the gun carrier's wheels hit a tree, sending the two unfortunate soldiers flying through the air.

The planes flew away, leaving a trail of wounded soldiers and devastation. For a while we were all still too frightened to emerge from the shelter of the trees as ammunition was still exploding all around us. Eventually my father ran to see if he could be of any assistance to the two soldiers who had come off their horses. He found, however, that one was already dead and the other could not move. My father gave him a drink of water and then ran towards the road, hoping to find some help.

STORM CLOUDS

Ten minutes later he came back with two cavalry men who had lost their horses in all the commotion. They carried the soldier towards the road, one holding his head, the other his legs, while my father supported his waist. The soldier was screaming in agony. After several minutes my father came back to us looking very upset, and told us that we were getting out of this inferno. We collected our things together and started walking.

Still able to hear the explosions coming from the train, we kept to the side roads in case the planes came back again. By now I had started to get nervous every time I heard a plane in the distance. The Germans flew the skies with impunity, no Polish Air Force to be seen, no anti-aircraft artillery to be heard. We walked through some orchards and picked some fruit as we were getting low on food. There was very little bread left and as there were no shops in the villages, we had to make haste for Lask where we hoped to buy some provisions before dusk.

At last the town came into view. Everything looked so peaceful, but we found, when we got there, that the shops were closed. Our first task was to find a place to sleep and to wash and to be able to put our luggage down. That, especially, seemed important; the longer we walked, the heavier our legs seemed to get. My father and I went in search of accommodation, leaving my mother, brother and sister behind with our belongings.

As we approached the market square, we stopped and asked a man if he could help us. He asked us where we had come from, so we told him and said we were hoping to go to Lodz. He couldn't think of a place to stay, but kindly offered us his home as it was getting late. He told us his name was Moshe Kaminski and that he was a tailor by profession, with six children.

A DETAIL OF HISTORY

My father accepted his kind offer and we collected the family together and followed him to his home. As we reached his door, we noticed that part of his house had collapsed and all the pebble dash was hanging off the walls. We entered the house and Mr Kaminski introduced us to his wife, explaining to her about our predicament. At first she was a bit perplexed, then she agreed to help, saying how unfortunate it was that people had to leave their homes because of the war. They had no electricity. A nafta lamp stood on the table, and their meagre belongings consisted of a treddle sewing machine in the corner of the room and two oval photographs hung on the wall, one of which was a picture of their wedding.

They looked so young and handsome in that photograph, he with his hair parted down the middle and sporting a large moustache, she a head taller than he, wearing a head-dress and veil. Though small in stature, we soon discovered that Mr Kaminski had a big heart. The second photograph was of him in a soldier's uniform with a soldier on each side.

One other photograph stood on the sideboard, depicting an elderly couple. The man in the picture had a long beard, whilst the lady wore a white shawl over her shoulders and looked very proud. I didn't ask, but assumed it must have been either Mr or Mrs Kaminski's parents.

I could hear giggling coming from the next room where all the six children slept in one double bed. Mr and Mrs Kaminski slept in a single bed. There were just two rooms and a kitchen in the house, no bath, just a toilet in the yard. We washed ourselves from a jug and bowl. That night we all slept on the floor, but it was better than the open air.

Next morning my brother and I stood for two hours in a queue to get bread, and ran back afterwards because it was getting late.

STORM CLOUDS

We thanked Mr and Mrs Kaminski for allowing us to stay overnight in their home, and my father left them some money for their trouble. Then we set off again, making for Pabianice where my sister Mania lived. This time we walked at the side of the main roads, as everything appeared to be calm. After a while we rested, during which time the Polish army passed us by, coming from the direction of Sieradz. They were in a terrible shambles - soldiers walking wounded, some with bandages on, others lying on carts drawn by horses. We all felt very sorry for them. We stopped at a village, where we saw a bus with people embarking. The sign above it said that it was going to Pabianice. We didn't hesitate for a moment and climbed aboard, happy and relieved that we didn't have to walk any more that day. Within half an hour we were in *Ulica Buzniczna*, where my Aunt Hela and Uncle Benjamin lived.

We were greeted by Aunt Hela (my father's sister), my Uncle Benjamin and my sister Mania, who lived with them and whom we hadn't seen for a long time. What a wonderful reception they gave us, full of hugs and kisses. We each had a bath, food was prepared, and the next day I went for a walk with my brother around the town of Pabianice. Everything was relatively quiet here, with no sign of war at all. It was an industrial town, textile mills very much the predominant industry. When we told our relatives what we had been through up to arriving in Pabianice, they looked at us with amazement. Here people walked in the streets, the shops were open and everything was normal.

After staying with our relatives for two days, father decided we should move on to Lodz, our final destination, where some of our other cousins lived. We said our goodbyes, then took a tram around the corner from our relatives. My sister Mania took us to the station, kissed us goodbye, and we were on our way once again.

A DETAIL OF HISTORY

We had to stand on the tram as it was packed with people. I remember we passed numerous grey ugly buildings. After journeying for an hour, we arrived in the city of Lodz.

Lodz was a large, ugly, industrialised city, with a pre-war population of about 700,000 people. It had textile mills and many smaller factories, which produced a variety of different products similar to those of pre-war Manchester in England. Jews played a prominent part in the commercial running of the city of Lodz.

We made our way to *Ulica Polnocna* - West Street - where our relatives owned a dairy. We received a lovely reception from our cousins, and several friends came to see my parents. Here everything was peaceful; business went on as usual. People were talking about the war, but so far Lodz was untouched by it - no bombing, no battles. Mother took all three of us to look around the shops, where we saw Jewish people discussing business in Yiddish as though nothing was happening.

However, that night we were woken by heavy aerial bombardment. We could hear the familiar frightening sounds gradually moving nearer and nearer. Everybody got out of bed, some naked, some in their nightclothes. People began running out into the street from all three floors as the building was a tenement. They congregated in my cousin's flat, asking for advice. Should they go in the direction of Brzeziny, they wanted to know, a town on the way to Warsaw. Many made that journey only to be killed by German planes.

The fifth column were very active in these parts, directing people to certain places, where they were caught out by the German fighter planes who brought panic to the population. Though many left Lodz, my father decided that we would stay, that we had travelled as far as we were going.

STORM CLOUDS

Gradually the bombing subsided and everything became quiet once more. The Germans knew that they didn't have to bomb the city, they could quite easily take it intact. Next morning I went out of the building, where I noticed people running towards *Platz Wolnosci* - Freedom Square. I followed the crowd, wanting to know what was going on. After watching for several minutes, I noticed a number of motorbikes with side cars, travelling very fast. These bikes were being driven by German soldiers dressed in grey leather long-coats and helmets. This was my first realisation that the Germans had finally arrived and I ran home to my relatives and parents to tell them the news.

The next day I watched the might of the German army marching into Lodz; an incredible sight which lasted hours. There were columns of soldiers with heavy artillery pieces, some drawn by horses, others by motors. There was division after division of motorised infantry in armoured vehicles, and there were planes flying overhead. I was overwhelmed by the weaponry and the discipline of this army, like a huge, well-oiled machine advancing inexorably on Warsaw.

On the third day I saw German officers catching Jewish men and burning or cutting their beards off. They were laughing and being photographed in the process. 'Such barbarism,' I thought. This was my first taste of German brutality and their attitude to the Jews.

After watching such horrific scenes, my father decided to return with our family to Sieradz. Little did we realise there were far worse things to come into all our lives. We took our leave, saying goodbye to our cousins and friends in Lodz. Everybody agreed we would be better off in a small town.

The journey back was by bus, which took us past Lask and Zdunska Wola. The roads were full of German troops going towards

A DETAIL OF HISTORY

Lodz and then Warsaw. Their columns seemed never ending. On the sides of the roads, I could see crosses with German helmets on them, hundreds upon hundreds. Not a single Polish one did I see throughout the journey from Lodz, and I presumed from this that as far as the Germans were concerned, it didn't matter where the Poles were buried.

At last we arrived back in Sieradz, so much having happened that it seemed like a whole year had passed. We found many of our belongings had been plundered, though the crates of fruit that we had left in the cellar remained intact. My parents quickly set to work, selling them off before they could go bad.

It felt now as though our lives were starting to return to normal again. It seemed nothing else mattered as long as we were all together back home and alive. Next day I ran to see if my cousins were all back, and was delighted to find my uncles Pesach, Natal, and Moshe too, had returned in one piece with their families. We quickly caught up on the news; each of us having different stories to relate of the past two weeks. One worry was that the Judkiewieczs had not returned yet, and we all hoped that they were well.

Soon after we returned to Sieradz, I was caught in the market square, and together with many more Jewish men was made to dig up bodies of German soldiers killed in the battle around Sieradz and put them into coffins. I was horrified by what I saw - decomposed bodies, some without arms or legs which had been blown off. It was a terrible experience for me, the true horrors of war, and it had a great impression on my later life. From that time I have always believed it is better to talk than to cut each other to pieces in battle. I only wish that the statesmen of this world would think the same way.

STORM CLOUDS

The Germans were now beginning to round up Jewish men in the streets for work. On many occasions I saw these men being beaten up for no apparent reason. I was caught several times and made to unload wagons of coal and briquettes (compressed coal dust). In the first winter, I remember working with French prisoners of war and later on with British. We had problems conversing with each other, as none of the prisoners spoke German, Polish or Yiddish, so we developed a form of sign language. I was sorry for the prisoners of war because they were guarded by German soldiers with guns, whereas we were still free to a certain extent.

At that time, the Jewish children were deprived of their education as the Germans had closed our school. Standing by the main highway one day, very near to our closed school, I watched the German army convoys travelling towards Lodz, probably bound for Warsaw. I was amazed at the size of artillery guns and the large quantities of weapons. The Polish army had nothing to match it, and I thought it was no wonder the German army had taken Poland in such a short time. Our army had never been trained for such a *blitzkrieg* - 'lightning war'.

Once again, Sieradz became an army garrison town. Newly-built barracks and training facilities had been left intact by the Polish army when they withdrew, and now the Germans were using them for their own training. One day I watched the German army columns marching down our street on their way to manoeuvres, singing, *"Wir gehen gegen England"* - "We are marching against England."

England, which was to become my home in later years, then seemed a foreign, faraway place. I reflected, however, that it must have been important for the Germans to feel they had to sing about it.

A DETAIL OF HISTORY

When the Germans first occupied Poland, there was still a chance for Jews to cross into Russian-occupied Poland outside Bialystok. Thousands of Jews and Christian Poles made the journey, but my father failed to make a decision quickly enough.

I remember a conversation in which he said the Germans weren't that bad in the First World War, but I now realise that that was an illusion that some people kidded themselves with. Perhaps this is why I began to value decisiveness. When an opportunity arises, I believe it should be taken quickly. My father was a good man; he trusted in God, he did his duty towards his religion, his family and his country. Perhaps, in spite of the history of persecution of the Jews, he could not envisage the evil which was about to be unleashed. This is one of the many things I was never to have the opportunity to discuss with him. My Aunt Hela and Uncle Benjamin left for Russia, where we had some relatives, and because of their foresight survived the war.

I remember people coming to my father for help in hiding their money and valuables when they crossed the border. He used to make a hole in the heel of his boot, filling it with paper money and jewellery, then covering it with leather or rubber. I was hoping that my father would take us on the same road to Russia, but when he did finally decide it was too late - the border was already closed. Our fate was sealed. The butchers were planning in the meantime how to liquidate the Jews of Poland and Europe. They plundered houses, shot or hanged hostages, and rounded people up in the streets like animals. One had to hide not to be caught. Professional people in high pre-war positions were taken away and shot for no apparent reason.

One example of this sort of treatment in our town happened one day when we were all sitting round the table having lunch.

STORM CLOUDS

Suddenly we heard the sound of jackboots marching in the street, and thinking that the German army was undertaking manoeuvres, I dashed to the door to watch. What I saw however, sent a chill through me. Soldiers were stopping at every door, four armed men to each house. It was obvious their intentions were hostile. I shouted to my father and my brother Tovia to hide, and I myself dashed up to the pigeon loft where I could observe more clearly what was going on. Disturbed pigeons flew everywhere at my panicked entrance, but the loft provided a very good vantage point.

I saw German soldiers dragging Jewish men from their houses, and kicking and beating them in the street; with horror I noticed that my father was among them. The Jewish men were forced to run towards the market place, where two rows of armed German soldiers were waiting for them.

They then had to run through the German gauntlet where they were savagely kicked and clubbed with rifle butts. My cousin Idle Natal, only twenty-one years old, was kicked to death in this melee.

All the men were then taken to the army barracks and held there overnight. The Germans, it transpired, were accusing some Jewish men of firing at a German soldier, and not knowing who was responsible, were holding all Jewish men as hostages until the culprit owned up. Fortunately, a Polish Christian woman happened to have seen the shooting, and she went to the German police and told them the truth. It eventually came to light that it had been a Polish Christian, and not a Jew at all, who had carried out the shooting in a moment of drunkenness.

After this incident all the men were released from the barracks, some with broken arms and legs. My father got off lightly with a few bruises.

A DETAIL OF HISTORY

Thus ended a terrible and tragic episode in our town. My cousin was dead and many others had been crippled for life. And all because the Germans couldn't be bothered to find out the true facts.

German soldiers amuse themselves by intimidating
this Jew and cutting his beard.

THE WAR BEGINS
Growing old fast: age eleven

At the beginning of the war the Germans decided to set up a
committee and a Jewish police force to supervise the Jewish part
of the town, as most of them lived in a close community and it gave
them a feeling of more security. The committee performed a
service for the Germans by supplying a Jewish labour force. At
that time they only needed men to work locally.

My parents were earning a good living selling fruit; they had
some good suppliers who grew their fruit in the surrounding
villages. Everything was done openly and freely, but as time went
on things started to get more difficult to acquire. Food began
being rationed and cigarettes were practically impossible to obtain
and were at a premium.

One day I was standing in the market square, watching some
German soldiers smoking and throwing away half-smoked
cigarettes, when a great idea suddenly occurred to me. I dashed

home and found a box, and armed with an old glove on my right hand I ran back to the spot and retrieved all the 'dimps' I could find. Soon my box was full. The next day I went to the army barracks which was situated about two kilometres from the town centre, and there I found hundreds of discarded cigarettes. I picked them all up and took them home. My next job was cutting the 'burnt' ends off. I was left with the clean tobacco, which I mixed very well. I then had to try and get some cardboard filters and a cigarette-making machine. I asked my father for some money and I went to all the shops to try and get my purchases, but after much searching I was still unsuccessful and was feeling very dejected. Then, to my good fortune, one shopkeeper told me that I would be able to get my filters from Zdunska Wola, which was about fifteen kilometres from Sieradz. When I told my parents, they were not too happy about allowing me to go all that way on my own, but I suggested that I could always go and see my relatives who lived there.

After much persuasion on my part, my parents relented, and I promised them that if I needed any help I could always go to my uncle and cousins. I was then just a young boy of eleven.

I put my money and the address where I would get the equipment in my pocket and started on my journey. I knew all the short cuts out of Sieradz and soon I was on the main highway, crossing the main bridge that spanned the river Warta. After walking for several kilometres I decided to remove my shoes, tie the laces and carry them around my neck. It was much lighter and quicker to walk without my shoes on.

There wasn't very much motorised transport on the roads at this time, mainly horses and carts. I decided that I would jump on the next cart that passed as I was now very tired. The driver noticed that I was hanging on and started to lash out with his whip. Needless to say, I jumped off very quickly and started to walk again.

At long last I reached Zdunska Wola, and, after a passer-by had directed me to the street I wanted, soon found the shop I was looking for. I bought five hundred filters and the cigarette-making machine, which I put in my shirt. To be seen carrying parcels at that time created suspicion, but being a small boy nobody took much notice.

So eager was I to get back to my home and settle down to manufacture my cigarettes that I didn't call on my relatives. I started my journey back, hitching a lift from a kind peasant. There was public transport going between towns, but it was too dangerous for Jews to use it. My parents were delighted to see me back home, and soon I was in bed, worn out from the day's journey.

I awoke next morning, refreshed and eager to start my cigarette making. I produced about four hundred perfect-looking cigarettes that I knew I could sell with very little trouble. I put my cigarettes in the boxes ready to sell the next day, which, being Friday, was market day.

That Friday I stood on the corner of *Ulica Zamkowa* and the market square. I called the peasants into the forecourt and quietly showed them my cigarettes. One had to be very discreet as there was always the German police about and dealing in cigarettes was strictly forbidden. I sold out, and my customers asked me to bring more the following week.

Excitedly I dashed home to my parents to tell them how I had sold out and to give them the money I had earned. I kept enough money back to be able to purchase another supply of filters. I remember how very proud my parents were of me and my 'ingenuity.'

A DETAIL OF HISTORY

The next day I went back to the army barracks for more cigarette butts, and also everywhere else the Germans used to frequent. As the weeks wore on, I had to buy more and more filters, and, as a result, had to borrow a larger jacket from my brother to hide my parcels. I was doing fantastic trade, the supply not meeting the demand. However my supply of 'dimps' was by now getting lower and lower and I was becoming desperate for tobacco.

One day while out playing in the park with my friends, I noticed some yellow leaves on the trees and struck on an idea. I filled my shirt with the leaves and ran home. My friends thought I had gone crazy. "What on earth do you need leaves for?" they asked.

I had the idea that if I dried and chopped the leaves into little pieces and then mixed it with the tobacco, this would help me to meet the demand. However, after trying this method I found it to be of no use as the smell was just awful. I was not daunted. I went back to the park, found some other type of leaf and made a fresh mixture. This one appeared to be much better, and my customers seemed very satisfied with my new brand of cigarettes.

As time went on I became more daring, especially when I used to go shopping for the filters. One day as I was coming home from such an errand, and was taking my usual short cut, the inside of my shirt bulging with the filters, I suddenly realised that a German policeman called Artur was following me. I became alarmed as he had a reputation for being ruthless. He called out to me, "Stop or I will shoot." I turned round, saw he was about a hundred metres behind me, and started to run, hoping for the best. I knew I could run very fast despite the bulge of filters around my waist. Once again he called for me to stop or he would shoot. I started running in a zigzag fashion, then glanced back and saw that he had taken his revolver out of his holster. I was terrified, but kept on running, knowing that if I could turn the next corner I would be on my own territory where I knew every blade of grass and every brick of the buildings. After several turns I made it, thankful that he was hindered by his high officer's boots which were difficult to run in.

I knew I could not go straight home as he would have found me immediately, so I decided to go to a smallholding which was owned by a man who had two horses, several goats and a few sheep. I dashed into an empty stable, out of breath, only hoping that the policeman had not noticed which way I had gone. Looking to my left, I saw to my horror rats the size of cats running around. I was terrified, but dare not call out in case I was still being searched for. After half an hour I decided to take a chance and come out of hiding. I ran all the way home, and when I told my parents of the day's events, they told me that I must not go to Zdunska Wola to buy my filters any more. My cigarette business continued for some time longer, but without the filters the cigarettes were not as good and I eventually gave it up.

One day, out of the blue, the Jewish committee were given an order from the German authorities. They required two hundred strong men to send away to work. As Sieradz did not have a large Jewish community, it quickly became clear that everybody would feel the loss of these men very acutely. I remember only too well Itzchak, Rozenstein, Harlupski, Yacob Herszkowicz, Zygier, Kutner, all the cream of our youth, some teenagers, other young men in their twenties. They were told to register with the Jewish committee and were then given a date on which to assemble. This done, they were then transported to a camp near Poznan in Poland.

After a time they were allowed to send back the odd letter, which was naturally censored, and every so often parents or wives were allowed to send food parcels. We were all under the impression that these men were not having such a bad time, but in point of fact they received a terrible hammering. The work was extremely hard and they were subjected to awful beatings. However, as the mail was censored nobody knew the real truth.

Several months passed and then the Germans requested more men. The committee had to pick some older men this time because most of the teenagers had gone on the earlier transports. On this occasion nobody was notified in advance, everything was done secretly. The Germans in conjunction with the Jewish police woke people up during the night and the men were taken from their beds. One night there was a knock on our door and a German policeman, followed by a Jewish policeman, asked my father to get dressed and go out into the courtyard to wait with a group of men already rounded up. My mother asked the Jewish policeman what was going on, and he replied that more men were needed to work in the labour camps.

My father got dressed, said goodbye to my mother, kissed us children and left. We were all numb with shock. Why did they have to do it during the middle of the night? Why couldn't they have done it during the day? My father went out into the courtyard.

About ten minutes later, the German policeman burst into our house, screaming at my mother, "Where did your husband go?"

My mother replied, "He went out in front of you and that was the last I saw of him."

Still screaming, the policeman demanded, "Who else is here?"

"My sons, Tovia and Arek," my mother said.

The policeman then demanded that my brother, Tovia, get dressed immediately. He was four years my senior. Tovia got dressed, said goodbye to us all, and walked out. We were all extremely upset.

THE WAR BEGINS

After about half an hour our front door was once again kicked open by the same German policeman who was in the most terrible rage. He demanded of my mother, "Where is your son?"

My mother said, "I don't know. He walked out in front of you and I haven't seen him since."

Suddenly the policeman pointed at me and ordered me out of bed and told me to get dressed. He said to me, "Your brother and father have escaped, so you will have to go in their place." My mother pointed out that I was only a child, just eleven years of age. He said, "It doesn't matter. He will have to go just the same."

As far as I was concerned I wasn't too bothered, as I thought I would be back home next day because I was so young and small. My mother cried and kissed me goodbye. In the morning we were taken to the army barracks on the outskirts of town. We were ordered to undress and we had a medical to make sure that we were fit enough for work. The man that was next to me was called Gertler, he was a member of the Jewish committee. When the doctor saw me he commented to Gertler that really I was far too small to be sent out labouring. Gertler informed him that my father and brother had escaped and that was the reason why I was present. The doctor stamped my card and from that point my fate was sealed. I had resigned myself to the fact that there was no other option open to me. I thought to myself, 'Maybe because I'm so small I might have a better chance of survival. They might just give me a lighter job.'

We were in the army barracks most of that day, but towards the evening we were all assembled and marched towards the railway station. Many of the boys that were with me were a few years older than myself, but I remember playing games with some of them, and a few were friends of my brother, Tovia. There was David, Mayer,

A DETAIL OF HISTORY

Shaja, Moniek, Beniek and many others. When we arrived at the station I suddenly saw my brother, Tovia, carrying a suitcase and hiding in a corner, quietly beckoning me over to him. I approached him, making sure the German policeman hadn't noticed us. I asked why he had taken the risk of coming down to the station, and he told me that he was here to take my place and that he wanted me to go home. I refused, and though he tried to persuade me for an hour he finally realised that he could not change my mind. Tovia gave me the suitcase and made me promise to be careful and write home as soon as I got to my destination. We said goodbye with tears in our eyes, then he disappeared. At that moment I felt a very big man indeed.

D

Hermetically sealed vans similar to this were used to murder Jews as they were transported to Chelmno death camp. Carbon monoxide was piped into the van where up to 80 people had been forced on each journey.

OTOSCHNO: CAMP OF DEATH
"Hope was all we had....."

We waited at the railway station in Sieradz until dusk. Suddenly a passenger train stopped, and we were told by the German police to proceed to the carriages at the back which were reserved for us. We were hurried along, I panting under the weight of my heavy case. I climbed aboard the last wagon, and a few minutes later the engine whistled, the locomotive belched, and we started to move. The train began to speed along, faster and faster, yet the journey was very tedious and I could not sleep. All through the night I was thinking about my family, hoping they wouldn't catch my father and brother and take them to another camp. My mind was in a turmoil; I was worried what was in store for us in the camp we were going to.

As dawn approached, the people in my compartment started to wake, tired and weary, everyone hoping and praying that we would soon be at our destination. The train was still speeding along, and looking through the window I saw farms, woods and trees, all situated on land that was very flat, no hills whatsoever. Suddenly the train began slowing down, and then came to an abrupt halt. Half an hour passed, then all at once we realised that our part of the train had been separated from the rest, and we were being coupled to another engine. Soon we were on the move again.

We travelled for several more hours before the train started to slow down and finally came to a halt. There were just a few wagons with the men from Sieradz. I looked out of the window and saw to my left a tiny brick-built station, and painted in black letters on a white background was the word 'OTOSCHNO'. Directly in front of me I saw several wooden prefabricated barracks. There were no trees, and a wire fence surrounded the area. People were walking around and there were some black-uniformed men.

I knew that at long last we had reached our destination.

Ten minutes elapsed, then a man in civilian clothing ordered us to disembark and told us to stand in rows like an army to be counted. After several minutes an elderly man appeared. He was somewhere in his sixties with a stoop and was not very tall. He wore a navy blue striped civilian suit, and was accompanied by two younger men in civilian clothing, who immediately began looking us over.

Suddenly the older man started talking to us in German, and what we heard we could hardly believe. He said, "Who out of the older men and boys would like to go back home to your town? If you wish to go back, take two steps forward." I was one of the first to take 'two steps forward' and was soon followed by some more boys and older men.

The Germans told us to put our suitcases to one side and wait, then the older man ordered the remainder of the other group to

OTOSCHNO: CAMP OF DEATH

leave their cases standing at the station and start marching towards the camp, which was two hundred metres away. We did not realise that by taking those 'two steps' we had signed our death warrants. The older man turned out to be the camp commandant.

We waited on the railway platform and watched the others marching towards the camp. Suddenly the guards in the black uniforms started to scream at this column and began to lash out with their whips. They tried to make them run onto a board, only about one foot wide, placed on ground that was very muddy and full of clay. They began to beat the men at the back of the column, who in their panic tried to run forward, out of the way. This resulted in the men in the middle falling off the boards and thus being at the mercy of the guards. As the proceedings intensified, people began sinking into the mud and it quickly became chaotic. The screams of the people were terrible to hear; it was a scene of sheer pandemonium. It was like a terrifying nightmare as nobody had expected this kind of treatment.

Our turn came, and as we walked forward the guards repeated the performance. I got kicked and beaten, but I knew that at all costs I had to stay on the board and not fall into the sea of mud. If I did so I knew I would be at the mercy of these terrible guards, and if that happened I was lost.

After managing to survive this dreadful ordeal, we were taken to a different barrack from the men who had been selected for work. Our barrack was empty, no chairs or seats, just loose straw for us to sleep on. Despite the way we had been treated, at this time we were still thinking that we were going to be sent home.

During the night I was in great pain from the kicks and beating that I had received. The guards were not too particular where they kicked you, and I had many whip marks on my body.

A DETAIL OF HISTORY

There was no medical help, and that first night was sheer hell for everybody in our barrack. The pain was so bad I could not sleep. There were older men and young boys in the barrack, moaning and groaning from the pain. Never mind, I thought, at least we will soon be going home to our families. Little did we know at that stage just what was in store for us.

Next day, limping along, I walked towards the next barrack. There was not a blade of grass or a tree in sight, just clay and mud and planks of wood to walk on. There were four wooden barracks in all, and a wash-house which had cement troughs in which everybody had to wash. We had to use pans of water as there was no pumped water in the camp.

There were two brothers living next to us in their early twenties, one called Abraham and the other David. David was made foreman as they had been in the camp several months. David said they were constructing a new railway line, and in the course of our conversation he mentioned that he came from a town called Konin. I told them that I had lived there for several years, and it transpired that the brothers knew most of my relatives, which struck a bond between us right away. They told me that the work was hard, that they were given very little food and that the guards were extremely brutal.

One foreman called Rudi, who was in charge and who came from Sudetenland in Czechoslovakia, was particularly brutal. I remember he was blond, of medium build and he wore glasses. He killed prisoners by hacking them to death with a spade. He was indeed one of the worst barbarians in the camp.

Our working day lasted for fourteen hours. For many workers life became so bad that they threw themselves under passing trains as they could not take any more. Many others were hanged for the

OTOSCHNO: CAMP OF DEATH

most trivial things, such as begging for a potato in the village or walking away from a work column to urinate without asking the guard's permission. The excuse that the guards gave was that they thought the prisoner was trying to escape.

Starvation was another terrible problem. The workers were given only one small piece of bread, some black coffee and a little watery soup each day. There were ceaseless terrible beatings on the ramp until the person was near death. All this summed up the terrible existence of most of the prisoners in this hell of a camp, but to us in our barrack we had hope because we thought we were going home.

One day David, the foreman, said to me, "Why don't you stop here? You could get an easy job, maybe working in the kitchen. You are the smallest and I'm sure I can help you. Maybe you could get a job peeling potatoes or something similar."

I was grateful for his kindness, but I wasn't about to listen to him. After all, I was going home to my family; the camp commandant had said so. I realise now that he obviously knew something at that time that I didn't, but he didn't know how to warn me. Once more he tried to convince me by saying, "You once lived in Konin. You are like one of us. We have something in common." I still ignored him.

A few days later a high-ranking German SS officer arrived from Wrzesnia, a large town near Otoschno. All the young people from my barrack were ordered to come out, assemble in the yard and form into rows. The officer then proceeded to walk up and down, looking very hard at us as he passed. When he had done this a few times he stopped and spoke to us. He said, "Which of you boys would like to stop here and work in the kitchens?" None of us made a move. Who in their right mind would want to stay in this hell when we had all been told we were going home? Once again the officer repeated his question and once again nobody came forth with an answer. He then informed us that he would be back the next week.

A week passed and sure enough he was back, and still he got no volunteers to stay. Suddenly he pointed to two boys and said, "You and you, out!" He then pointed to me and several other boys and ordered us out and said, "From now on you are all going to work in the kitchen and you will help to bring water into the camp. You will move into the next barrack with the other working people. The rest of you boys go back into your barrack, you will go home."

At that point I was extremely upset, but little did I realise that the officer had just saved our lives. In the evening I met David the foreman and I told him what had happened, and his reply was that it was for the best.

There was no water laid on in the camp and that meant all the water had to be brought in from the village five kilometres away. The Germans provided us with a long metal container on four wheels and we were given the job of hauling this water tank to and fro. It was really work for a team of horses, but why use animals when there was an abundance of human beings to do the work?

The Germans roped some teenagers together onto the cart and we hauled this contraption several times a day. I was chosen as one of the boys to do this work. We were guarded by the black-uniformed men who had whips in their hands, and who every so often would lash out with them. Every day the guards were changed, but it never made any difference to their savagery. These black-uniformed guards were the worst barbarians I have ever come across.

However, there was one particular guard who would tell me to unrope myself and walk next to him, the reason being that I was the smallest and somehow he must have felt sorry for me. He also asked the other guards, all ethnic Germans who spoke Polish, to do the same thing. The situation in the camp got a little easier for me, and though the guards were still all very cruel, I became less frightened of them.

Another job I did was working with many other prisoners on the Poznan-Warsaw railway line, laying lines and sleepers. This work was terrible, back-breaking for even the fittest of men, and the beatings we received were so savage that many actually died from them.

On occasion the camp commandant would send me on errands, make me clean his room, polish his shoes or bring him water. He was a small man in his sixties, perhaps five feet three inches tall. He had a slight stoop, grey hair, wore glasses and was very cruel. He used to glean a special delight out of seeing prisoners being hanged and out of making the rest of us watch. He never spoke to me directly, simply shouted his orders, and when he wanted to call me he never used my name, but addressed me as 'you.' In all the time I knew him, I never once saw him smile.

Whenever I got the chance, I would visit the boys and older men who were waiting to go home. I was very envious of them and I asked them to give my mother my love and to tell her I was all right and that she should not worry about me.

The hangings started to increase, events which, as I said, we all had to watch. Life in the camp started to get worse as the rations of food grew less and less and the work became harder. Some of the prisoners started showing signs of malnutrition and were dying. There was just one medical man for the whole of the camp, and he did not have any drugs so there was very little he could do to help his fellow men. In short, life was a living hell.

One afternoon as I was walking towards the wash house, I noticed some strange-looking lorries that had arrived at the camp.

A DETAIL OF HISTORY

These vehicles were all enclosed and were manned by soldiers who had their sleeves rolled up and carried sticks in their hands. These soldiers had SS on their collars, and a skull and crossbones insignia on their hats. The lorries were driven to the block that housed the boys and men waiting to go home. They stopped, and the SS men ordered the prisoners out of the barrack and told them to undress, but to leave their underpants on. The prisoners obeyed immediately and the backs of the lorries were then opened up. The SS then proceeded to beat the boys and men onto the lorries.

The screams and panic which broke out at this treatment were just too terrible. Many were bleeding from the blows that had rained down on them. When everybody was inside the lorries, the doors were closed.

Days later I found out from the foreman that as the engine started running it began to pump the exhaust fumes into the back of the lorry. As the vehicle was airtight, this meant that all inside were slowly gassed. Though I didn't realise it at the time, I still don't think I will ever be able to erase the memory from my mind of that terrible day when I unwittingly witnessed the deaths of my friends. I still shudder when I think that if I hadn't been picked out with those other few boys to work, that would have been my fate too. As more and more people were hanged, one of my duties was to help take the corpses down to the little village which was several kilometres from the camp, where we would help to bury them. I still remember the spot.

I had a friend in Sieradz called Beniek who was my age. He had an elder brother, Shymek, who had been caught begging for a potato. We were ordered to watch Shymek being hanged in the wash house. Twice those brutes hanged him and twice the rope snapped, and each time, in a dreadful state of shock, he begged for his life. However, those barbarians succeeded the third time.

OTOSCHNO: CAMP OF DEATH

That incident typified the bestiality of the Germans and their extermination methods in the beginning. I was heartbroken as I watched this terrible scene, and afterwards I helped to bury him. He was only twenty years of age, a very intelligent person and one of the nicest young men anybody could wish to know. Here I was, a young child of just thirteen years of age, and already I had witnessed some of the most inhuman acts that man had done to man in recent history.

It was now October, 1941. On my many errands that I was ordered to do for the camp commandant, I went several times to the railway station. I remember watching the Red Cross trains passing through Otoschno station full of wounded German soldiers coming away from Russia, and also rolling stock which were carrying tanks and other types of heavy equipment. I also saw Italian and German soldiers being taken to the Russian front. I used to hope when I watched all this activity that maybe very soon the war would be over. Hope was all we had.

Winter was now upon us and the Polish winters are very severe. There was very little fuel to be had in the camp and the death toll started to mount alarmingly. People had no resistance to the terrible cold. I remember seeing my friends, Mayer, David, Shaya and Moniek walking through the camp, frozen with cold and very dejected. What hell it was; we spent all our time wondering just how long we would survive in these conditions. Many prisoners began to get swollen from lack of food and lack of fat. It was pitiful to watch some of the men.

Slowly spring arrived, and for boys like myself there was no religious education, no Hebrew schooling, not even a book to read. My parents had had such high hopes for me, they had planned a higher education and hoped I would one day go to university. Now all these hopes were just an illusion. My only concern now was to survive.

As the weather began to get warmer, my duties lasted for more hours in a day as I had to clean many rooms for the guards. In Sieradz the Germans were intensifying their roundup of Jews to send to work in Poznan and the surrounding areas, and this time my father was caught. I received this piece of news from a letter that my mother sent me. I was never to hear from my family again as all letters were censored. It gave me some satisfaction to know that my father had been at home for a year and that my family had been comforted by his presence, but now he had been taken away from my mother and life must have been very hard.

The summer passed, another winter came, more people threw themselves under the trains. For those poor souls life had become just too unbearable.

The spring of 1942 arrived, and still when I went on my errands past the railway, I could see there was no decline in the number of wounded soldiers coming from the Russian front and of trains going to Russia with more armaments and troops. We did not receive any news from the outside world, though just watching those transports gave us some indication as to what was going on at the Russian front. It appeared to us that the Germans were getting a good beating. I used to think that maybe the Germans would start treating us a little better, but that was just a pipe dream. I was now nearly fouteen years of age.

One day as I was cleaning the camp commandant's office, he was sitting at his desk reading some papers. He turned his head towards me, his gold-rimmed spectacles resting on the tip of his nose. He placed the papers he was reading on his desk and spoke to me. "You, I am sending you home," he said.

OTOSCHNO: CAMP OF DEATH

I looked at him in despair and my heart sank as I remembered what had happened to all my other friends who had been told they were being sent back to their families. He continued to speak and I listened, too fearful to believe that what I was hearing was true.

He told me that a man was arriving from Sieradz to take another boy home and that I could go as well. The other boy's name was Kuba Blum, whom I knew; he was working on the construction of a railway line. I wondered to myself why on earth we were being allowed to go home. The commandant told me that I was too small for work and this was the reason why he was allowing me to go as well. Now I began to feel that what this man was saying to me was genuine and much of my apprehension left me. He told me to go back to my block and return to the office at three o'clock with my belongings, which were very few, as everything had been taken away from us when we arrived. I was so excited; how wonderful to be able to see my mother and family again. I said goodbye to a few people, and everybody was envious of my going home.

I arrived at the office at three o'clock, knocked on the door and waited until I was commanded to enter. In the office stood a man that I'd known before the war, who earned his living by painting people's houses. Standing next to him was the boy I knew as Kuba Blum. I now knew for certain that what the camp commandant had told me previously was true. The last of my apprehension left me and I felt my heartbeat slow down to a normal tempo. The man was given our papers, and he suggested to Kuba and me that we should start our journey to the station as we did not have much time before the train was due. We started to walk to the station, but before I left the camp I looked back with much remorse for the unfortunate people who were left behind in that hell. In their wildest dreams, nobody could ever imagine what a terrible place that camp was.

A DETAIL OF HISTORY

After waiting several minutes the train arrived and we boarded it, and as we wore civilian clothes nobody questioned who we were. There were several Germans in our compartment, one of whom was reading a paper. This German looked at Kuba and me over his spectacles as we spoke together in Polish. For most of the journey, however, I talked to Herr Schmidt, the man who was taking us home. Kuba was not a talkative boy, he was always very quiet, but even he could not conceal his great excitement in our good fortune.

I couldn't wait for the moment when I would arrive back in Sieradz and see my family again. I sat back in my seat, unable to get over how lucky we were. However my thoughts kept on taking me back to Otoschno and to how badly we prisoners were treated. One would never think we were breathing the same air as the Germans. I remember the marches we were forced to do through a big town called Wrzesnia just near Otoschno. As we marched through the town for delousing, what a pitiful sight we all must have been, but the civilians just looked at us as if we were animals. The evil of the guards, the hunger and frustration, the prisoners swollen from starvation, the terrible beatings, being made to watch your own friends being hanged for no other reason than because they had begged for a potato. All these thoughts crowded into my mind as the train started to pick up speed on our homeward journey.

Herr Schmidt had brought some meat sandwiches with him and he gave us two each. They tasted marvellous. It had been such a long time since we had tasted anything like them.

The train started to pull into a station called Kutno. Before the war it had been an army garrison town like Sieradz. I was not expecting anybody to meet us at our destination as Jews were only allowed out of the ghetto for work. Every Jew had to wear a yellow

OTOSCHNO: CAMP OF DEATH

Star of David on his or her clothing, in the centre of which was the word *Jude* - Jew. If a Jew had permission to leave the ghetto he or she would have to walk in the middle of the road, as walking on the pavement was not permitted.

We journeyed on for hours, but I now recognised the names of the stations we were passing through. Kuba Blum still could not get over the shock of going home. I said to him, "Just imagine a clean bed, some food, nobody giving you a beating, and living like a human being again. How lucky we both are."

At last we arrived in Sieradz station, where nothing appeared to have changed. Herr Schmidt took the only kind of transport that was about at that time, a *droshke*. We went past the market square, then the cab turned into *Ulica Zamkowa* where Kuba and I lived. This street now formed part of the Sieradz ghetto, which was not fenced in, but which had Jewish police guarding the corner of each street. There were no Christians living in this part of the town now, only Jews, many of whom had been brought in from the town's outskirts. The synagogue here was no longer allowed to function; the Germans were now using it as a grain warehouse.

We pulled up at Kuba's house and thanked Herr Schmidt for everything, then we alighted from the cab. I shouted my farewell to Kuba and started to run like mad for my own home, which was about a hundred yards further down the street. I knocked on the door, which was opened by Tovia, my brother.

He was so shocked when he saw me, he just couldn't believe it. When my mother came to the door she nearly fainted with disbelief. Oh, how we hugged and kissed one another, my mother and my sister Itka crying with happiness. At first they thought I had escaped, but when I explained that I had been released they realised my return was genuine. Before I could get my breath back, half the ghetto people

A DETAIL OF HISTORY

were outside the house, all wanting to know if I had news of husbands, sons and their relatives. I was nearly crushed as groups of twenty people at once pushed towards me, asking if members of their own families were still alive.

And so ended a most terrible chapter in my life. In the period 1940-42, thousands of Jews of all ages went into that camp, of whom only eleven survived - Kuba Blum, myself and nine others. Otoschno was a small camp near the Poznan region which not many people had heard of, but in these small camps, terrible atrocities were perpetrated by the Germans. As soon as these places had fulfilled their function they were demolished.

The Kloister Church at Sieradz where I saw my mother, sister Itka, brother Tovia, my uncles and aunties and the other Jews of our town for the last time. In 1942 when the ghetto was liquidated, they were all assembled here and the next day taken to Chelmno and murdered.

THE LONELY ROAD TO LODZ
Separation at Sieradz

Amongst my family's non-Jewish friends was a Polish Christian boy called Stasiek, with whom we had always done business. During the time we were in the Sieradz ghetto he managed to get supplies in to us such as poultry and other foodstuffs. Even though the ghetto was open and not fenced in, it was still very difficult to do this as the ghetto was guarded closely by the Jewish police, who stood at certain vantage points. These police just wore special caps and had no guns, but the German police were always nearby.

I went in and out of the ghetto frequently, in a way that it would not have been possible for an adult to do. As I was only a small boy, no one took much notice of me, so every time I got out I bought more provisions from the peasants.

At about five a.m. one morning we were woken by a knocking on the door. Such a thing at that time in the morning inspired dread. We were certain that the Germans had come again to take away Tovia or me. Mother put a light on and asked who was there, eventually pulling back the hatch and peering outside. We were all surprised to see Stasiek, who came into the house and told us that he had come to warn us.

He had heard from some source which he trusted that all the ghetto inhabitants were to be liquidated that day. He urged us to run away, saying that if we started immediately there might still be time to escape.

My mother thanked Stasiek for the information he had brought and we each in turn said our goodbyes to him. It was obvious to all of us that he had taken a grave risk in attempting to save our lives. However, despite his warning, escape was not simple; there was nowhere for us to go. My mother reasoned that it would be better for us to stay and take our chance, and if the worst came to the worst we would at least be with the rest of the Sieradz Jews.

We all thought that if what Stasiek had said was accurate, the worst that might happen was that we should all be transported to a work camp. At that time my mother did not think that this would be too bad a fate; after all, my father was in a camp near Poznan and he was still alive, and I, who had been in a camp, had been sent home alive only two weeks before. Not wishing to alarm her, I said nothing, but my mind could not help turning back to what I had seen at Otoschno. We all thanked Stasiek again and then we said goodbye to him for the last time.

THE LONELY ROAD TO LODZ

At eight in the morning we all had to go to the *Apel Platz* - open ground - near to the unfinished school, five minutes walk from our house. We took with us what few belongings we could carry. All the Jews from Sieradz gathered on this open ground, row after row of us, where we were counted by the German police. I was only thirteen years old, but by this age I had learned to think for myself. I knew that I must always watch and wait and be one step ahead. I knew from experience that the Germans only spared those who were useful - that is to say, those who were fit for work.

I myself was too small to be chosen for work, but I took comfort in the fact that my brother Tovia, who was then seventeen, and my sister Itka, who was eighteen, were not only older but were also taller. This meant that their chances of being chosen for work were good. I worried somewhat about the fact that Tovia had a stiff knee due to a football accident when he was ten years old, but this knee did not seem to hamper him too much, nor would it readily be seen as something which would stop him from working. My mother, too, was relatively young - only thirty-nine years old - and very healthy. I thought to myself, 'Work will be found for her too.' These thoughts were a relief to me. It seemed that I was the only one who was at risk.

We were all marched to the Kloister church, situated next to the theatre with a large forecourt. I looked at the theatre, remembering how often I had been there with my parents to see plays and shows and sometimes to attend meetings. Now, however, the building was used as a theatre no more. Like almost everything else in Sieradz, the Germans had closed that down too.

Sieradz was a small town and most of its men had already been taken away to work in camps. This left a population of about one thousand, four hundred Jews, all of whom were crushed into the church, hardly able to move or breathe. I was full of thoughts of survival as I went through the big gates, and when I saw the German policeman whom I had worked for standing on guard, I smiled and tried to talk to him. However, he ignored me. Then I noticed that standing next to him was a group of SS, all with the telltale insignia on their collars and hats - a skull with crossbones.

After a long hour in the church, we were told to go outside. As we walked out, two SS officers asked us what our trade was. Knowing that only those chosen for the workforce would survive, I responded immediately, "*Schneider*," which meant 'tailor.' This lie was wasted on the officers who told me to go along with my family.

'Well whatever happens now,' I thought to myself, 'at least we shall all be together.' This thought brought me happiness. I looked over at the other side of the courtyard and saw a group of about one hundred and fifty people who were being told to stand in front of the church square. Everyone else was told to go back into the church. Amongst the group outside were many teenagers and fit-looking adults. I had not been right in thinking that my mother and brother and sister would be selected, but I had been right in thinking that I would not. The one hundred and fifty were the ones who might survive. I stood in the Christian church, and although I knew that my own chances of survival were slim, I felt resigned to my fate and my feeling of happiness that I was going to be with my family persisted. There was silence in the church, I keeping my thoughts to myself, then my mother looked at the three of us and said, "Thank God we are together." My uncles, aunts and cousins all remained in the church with us; none of us had been selected for the courtyard with the other group.

After a time I became very thirsty and I asked my mother if she had something I could drink from. "I'll go and ask the guard for some water," I said. From our possessions she brought out a metal pan and gave it to me. "I'll only be a second," I told her.

As I approached the gate, I realised that there was some kind of commotion. I could see an SS officer once again calling out to people, asking them their trade. As I approached with the pan, he shouted at me, "What are you?"

I answered automatically, "*Schneider!*"

This time the response was different. He shouted the word, "*Raus!*" - "out!"

I did as he asked, and was told to join the group of one hundred and fifty people who were standing outside the square.

Now I was struck with horror and disbelief at what I had done. The SS man's question had taken me by surprise. I was only thirteen years old and very small for my age. I had never held a needle in my hand and I did not know one stitch from another. As I walked towards the selected workers, I looked back through the gate, praying that I might at least catch a glimpse of my beautiful mother and my sister and brother. As I walked, tears poured from my eyes. Sadness such as I had never known filled me. The pan which my mother had given me I still held in my hand.

Those of us who had been selected were then marched off to a police station. We were held there overnight, three to a cell, cramped and uncomfortable, no mattresses or beds, and only a bucket in which to urinate. We did not know where we would be taken to from there. I was certain that it would be somewhere where there was work; we were in too good a physical condition to be disposed of. I sat on the floor of the cell and wept bitterly, wondering what had happened to my family. My longing for them was intense and I wished that I had stayed with them. Others tried to calm me; "Don't worry," one man kept saying. Everyone else tried to assure me that my family had simply been taken to another camp.

Just when it seemed that night would never end, we heard the sound of cell doors opening. We waited, and eventually our own cell door was opened. We had to put any money and jewellery on the table outside the cell. "You will not be needing such things where you are going," we were told. We emptied our pockets; I had six photographs of my family, which I kept, and the metal pan with which I'd gone to fetch water.

We were marched from the police station to the railway station, where we were each given half a loaf of brown bread, the only food for our journey. We boarded a train bound for Lodz, a trip which took five hours as the train stopped very often. When we reached Lodz we were kept overnight in the wagons.

Next morning we were taken to the Lodz ghetto, which was fenced in. At the gates were Jewish policemen and outside were German police. All the people I saw in the ghetto were very thin and undernourished. Those of us who had just arrived from Sieradz were taken to some large blocks of flats and were accommodated around ten to a room.

I did not sleep at all that first night. My thoughts were full of my mother, Tovia and Itka. I thought too about my father, who I knew was in a camp in Poznan, and about my other relatives. I worried about what had befallen them all.

The next day I walked about, dazed and shaken, not knowing what to do or who to talk to. All the people I had come with seemed to be in a similar state. As the days went by, I watched every transport that arrived at the ghetto from the provinces, searching longingly for someone from my family. I hoped against hope that another batch of people would be brought in from

THE LONELY ROAD TO LODZ

Sieradz, but these hopes were never realised. I learned from other people that a decision had been made that day in Sieradz to increase the number of people chosen to work by thirty. The thirst which had driven me to go to the church gate to ask for water, and the fact that I had said that word, "*Schneider*," had made me one of those thirty extra people. It had enabled me to survive.

I went on and on looking for my family and telling myself that they must be alive. Later I was to discover that those who had been left in the church, including my mother, my sister and my brother, had all been taken to the Chelmno extermination camp and murdered.

I sat on the floor of the room we had been put into, which contained no furniture, only mattresses, and I cried and cried. I asked myself, "Why was I chosen for this?" I did not see myself as chosen to survive, but simply to exist on my own, with no one in the world to care about me. I tried to stay as close as possible to the other people from Sieradz with whom I had come to Lodz, but it soon became obvious that all were beset with their own worries. Like me, they were desperately trying to find out about their own relatives, and we were all weak with hunger and dejection. None of us knew what the next day would bring, apart from no comfort and little food. Everyone in that ghetto was starving.

On 18 April 1942, all children over the age of ten years were ordered to report for medicals in order to determine their fitness for work. On 20 July 1942, the "*Elderst*" of the Lodz ghetto, Chaim Rumkowski, ordered that all children over the age of ten must report for work.

On 1 September 1942, with the help of Jewish police, most hospitals were cleared of their patients. Early that morning the SS blocked the entrances to the hospitals, drove up with lorries, and within a short time had taken most of the patients away. In the confusion, however, several of them managed to escape, but there were mothers trying to save their children who were grabbed by the SS and taken in their place. They were all driven to one destination and for one purpose only - to be murdered, many of them shot on the spot. Almost two thousand patients were disposed of in this way.

Chaim Rumkowski, the leader of the Lodz ghetto, loved children, although he had none of his own. Before the war he had been in charge of an orphanage in Lodz. He was a powerful man whom everyone had to obey. He had several hundred Jewish policemen under his control, helping to enforce his orders. Due to him, about ten thousand children were found work. Those over the age of seventeen were regarded as adults. Children between the ages of ten and seventeen worked shorter hours, yet even so the work was exhausting and all of us were short of energy as we had too little to eat.

Soon after this an order came from the Germans that between eighteen and twenty thousand Jews were wanted for resettlement, and notices were put up in the streets. We, however, were not fooled. We knew by now that 'resettlement' was simply another word for death.

The Germans specified that they wanted people between the 5th and 12th of September 1942. The numbers should be made up of all children under ten years of age, all old people and the unemployed. At that time I did not work as I had not been in the ghetto long enough to have been allocated a job. Hearing whispers about 'resettlement' in the street, I decided to play safe. I did not know the surroundings of the place where I was staying, and so decided to look around; to get to know the terrain, as it were. In the yard at the back of the flats was a high wall which surrounded a cemetery. I gambled that if the Germans made a house-to-house search, they would not come into the cemetery at the same time. As it happened, this gamble paid off. As the next day approached, I could hear shooting from several blocks away. I also heard screams as the soldiers came nearer to our flats.

At that point I decided to make my move. I found a place where I could climb the wall and I decided to climb it there and then. As I jumped down from the wall, I landed on a stone and twisted my ankle, but by this time I was immune to pain as I was shaking with fear. I dragged myself towards a tombstone to hide, praying to God, "Please help me; save me. Do not let them send me for resettlement." I limped from gravestone to gravestone, trying to get further from the wall. I heard noises and I lay on the ground, desperately pleading, "Please God, don't let them catch me."

The cemetery was in *Ulica Rybna* - Rybna Street - where the *Holtz Galanterie* - wood factory - was. I stayed there, paralysed with fear. Eventually the shooting subsided and at length I heard the screams of either the children or their mothers. I waited until this had all died away, and only then did I come out from my hiding place.

My intuition about the cemetery as a safe place had been right. I tried to walk normally, telling myself, "At least I can breathe again, thank God." I went back to my room and lay down; the other people there told me that they had given me up, thinking I had been taken away.

I stayed in the flats for several days. On the day I went out, still limping from my ankle injury, I walked towards the square next to *Ulica Rybna*. I saw that there were ten men in the square hanging from gallows. The Germans left them there for two days for people to see.

Life in the ghetto became harder. There was less food and I got hungrier every day. Little by little, I began to lose all hope.

Sometimes I would look out through the fence which surrounded the ghetto, and I would see people on the outside, walking around and travelling on trams. I wondered why it was right that they were free and we were fenced in. All of us were suffering from the effects of starvation, some so much so that their bodies had begun to swell from lack of food.

One day as I was standing at this fence, I felt despair take a great hold on me, and I sat down on the street corner and started to cry. As I sat, weeping, I suddenly felt a hand on my shoulder, and looking up I saw a woman standing over me. She was about forty years old, tall with grey hair, and was dressed in a black coat with a fur collar. She asked me what the matter was and why I was crying, so I told her how I had been selected at the church gates, how I had come to the Lodz ghetto on my own, and how I had no parents or family and no one to turn to for help. She looked at me and then suddenly she took my hand. "Come with me," she said.

I Followed her. As we walked, she said, "If you like, you can come and live with me." She explained that she had a child of her own, a girl of fourteen who was named Sala. "You will be able to play with her," she said.

The woman and her daughter, Sala, lived several blocks away from the spot where she had found me. Her home was a couple of rooms in a two-storey building. As we walked up the stairs together, I felt a sudden feeling of 'belonging'. "Somebody cares for me," I told myself.

THE LONELY ROAD TO LODZ

We reached the top of the stairs and a girl greeted us. She was taller than me, with short black hair, large dark eyes and a nice smile. She was wearing a blue dress and a bow in her hair. "Mama, did you bring something back?" she asked.

"Yes," her mother said, "I have brought Arek. He is going to live with us as he has nobody else. Between the three of us we will manage somehow."

Their own room was medium-sized with two beds, a little furniture and a stove. Next door was an empty room which Mme Unikowska told me would be mine.

While I was there, the contents of the room consisted of a mattress, which I slept on, a chair and two buckets, one for coal and the other for me to urinate in as the toilet was two floors down in the yard and was very difficult to find during the night. There was no heat whatsoever in my new room, and as a result it was extremely cold and damp.

Although Mme Unikowska was not an unkind woman, I was by no means as well off as I had thought I was going to be; in fact, conditions were little better than in the flats. Mme Unikowska and her daughter both saw me as a kind of servant.

After several weeks of sleeping without covers in the damp room, bitterly cold from the Polish winter, I developed a chill in my bladder and could no longer hold my water. I started to wet the bed at night, sometimes without even realising I had done it. I was feeling very ill at this time, but did not dare tell Mme Unikowska of this in case she decided I could not stay.

She worked as a cook for the fire brigade, and on occasions managed to get some soup to bring home. She gave me the job of taking a special bowl, which she had made, to the hatch in the kitchen of the fire station. The kitchen server recognised this bowl, knew who it was for and filled it up. On several occasions Mme Unikowska gave me some, but more often she did not. All in all she was careless of my welfare. Slowly I became thinner and thinner, until eventually my bones protruded so much I resembled a skeleton.

Winter wore on, and one day Mme Unikowska sent me on an errand to a place several streets away to collect some briquettes of compressed coal dust. The sack of briquettes was very heavy, and I found I could hardly lift it, I was so weak. I persevered, fearful of disobeying her, as I was always afraid she would turn me out. As I dropped the sack in the street, a young boy of about my age came over to help me lift it onto my shoulders.

He asked, "Why are you carrying such a big sack?"

I told him, "Because if I don't obey, the woman I'm living with will turn me out, and I have nowhere else to go."

As time went by, the demands Mme Unikowska made on me increased. I realised she had taken me in not because she had any real pity for me, but so that I could serve her as a kind of slave. Even worse than this was the fact that on occasion, when she was out at work, Sala, her daughter, would give me orders such as, "Come to my bed," and "Take off all your clothes." She would say, "You must obey me as well as my mother."

In fact, Sala did all she could to humiliate me; I was a shy boy and I felt this humiliation deeply. I began to resent her even more than I resented her mother. I told myself that I must get away.

One day I was walking in the streets, glad to be free of Mme Unikowska and her daughter for a time, when I met another boy of about my age who began to talk to me. He asked me where I lived and about my family. I told him that my father was in a camp in Poznan, that my oldest sister had gone away for safety,

THE LONELY ROAD TO LODZ

and that I was not sure where my mother, my other sister and my brother had been taken.

In turn he told me about himself. His name was Motek, and he too had no parents. He lived in an orphanage and he was happy there. He spoke of his many friends in the orphanage and the way they were all well looked after. He said that in the orphanage all the children were able to study and that they had books. At this time he worked in a textile factory called Kaszuba, which was not far from the orphanage.

I looked at him and compared his healthy, well-covered body with my own starved frame. "Meet me tomorrow night outside the orphanage at seven thirty," he said. The idea of this excited me and I promised that I would be there.

The orphanage building was tall, grey and pebble-dashed, situated next to the Ghetto Court. The next night, as I approached it, I felt nervous. I saw that facing the building was the place where the Jewish workers every so often got recuperation and bonus suppers (*kolacje*). Motek met me outside as we had agreed. As we walked in, we passed children of around my own age who were nicely dressed and reasonably well-fed. The place was clean and there was some good furniture. My eyes lit up as I saw this nice new world. Once again I could be a normal child, I thought, I could enjoy the luxury of belonging and of being cared for.

Motek gave me information about the orphanage and instructions about applying to enter it. I applied and was accepted. I said goodbye to Mme Unikowska and her unpleasant daughter, and left with my only possessions - a few photographs of my dear family and the tin pan my mother had given me.

It was with delight that I began this new chapter in my life.

Jews from the surrounding area obey orders to move to the Lodz ghetto in 1940.

THE ORPHANAGE
A haven amidst my nightmare

When I first entered the orphanage I had to acquaint myself with the new environment. The first few days were spent getting to know the place and meeting the other children. I was put into a room with two other boys whose names were Heniek and Szymek. Heniek was fair- haired with blue eyes and a very pale complexion. He was small for his age and had a serious look about him. He told me how his parents, his two younger brothers and his sister had been taken away for 're-settlement' to Chelmno. This meant they were certainly dead as Chelmno was an extermination camp. During my time in the orphanage, I never saw Heniek smile once.

Szymek was in complete contrast to his roommate. He was dark- haired, taller and always full of hope. He was an optimistic boy who was often quite witty.

Both boys greeted me with, "Welcome to the orphanage." They showed me my chest of drawers where I put my one and only shirt, my underpants and the few remaining photographs of my family, which meant more to me than anything else in the world. We had one wardrobe between the three of us, but it only contained Szymek's jacket and Heniek's coat. I had nothing to put in it.

At first everything seemed strange to me; I had a bed of my own and a warm room. There was no more sleeping on a wet mattress in a freezing cold room, no more squalor, dampness and misery. I received some clean underwear and clothing and a decent pair of shoes. Everything was so much better and I was in the company of many children of my own age.

Our *kierowniczka* - headmistress - was about sixty. A small woman with a hunchback, she and her husband were in charge of running the orphanage. I was told that I would take my duties in rotation with the other children, and as time went by I was given a job in a textile mill called Kaszuba. This was a pre-war weaving and spinning mill that was situated at the edge of the ghetto.

I was assigned to a man who repaired the machinery, whose name was Abram. The noise from the machines was deafening, but after a while I got used to it. Abram was a very kind man; he tried as much as possible to avoid asking me to help him put the heavy warp of yarns into the machines as I had little strength and they were very heavy. However, despite his protection, I still had to learn this job. I hated it, but it was better than being sent away, which would have meant certain death.

After a few weeks had gone by, Abram started to send me to the kitchen to collect soup for him in a specially marked utensil. He had a girl friend who worked at the serving hatch in the kitchen. She recognised the utensil and knew who the food was for, and so she always filled it with extra soup.

THE ORPHANAGE

We in the orphanage received slightly better treatment than others in the ghetto. Chaim Rumkowski, the *Elderst* of the ghetto, had a great affinity with the orphan children and made sure that we were treated that little bit better. We all took our turns with our duties in the orphanage. I soon got to know many of the children and made a lot of friends.

We had regular meetings and discussions in the main hall of the orphanage and on one particular day the *Kierowniczka* gave us a talk on different points appertaining to life in the orphanage. Suddenly she called out my name: "Would Arek Herszlikowicz please stand up." She then proceeded to tell the children to take an example from me, for my obedience, behaviour, honesty and hard work. She added that starting from the following week I would help with the weighing out of the bread rations and the other provisions. This was a great honour, a very responsible job as every crumb of bread was like gold. However I was not given any extra privileges for doing these chores; I was still on the same meagre rations as the other children. I felt somewhat embarrassed but very proud at what the *kierowniczka* had said about me. It was now six months since I had entered the orphanage.

Although life was a little easier for me now, events which had happened in the past few years still haunted my mind. My nights were often filled with terrifying nightmares, from which I would wake shaking and sweating. One of these vivid dreams still sticks in my mind.

I dreamt that I was being chased by two black cats through dark narrow alleys in the pouring rain. I ran and ran, sweating with fear, towards a closed gate, but as I neared it I felt myself going up on a ladder, away from the gate. I kept on running, heading towards the sky, and a frightening mass of black clouds. As I turned my head,

A DETAIL OF HISTORY

I saw two SS men in black uniforms pursuing me. I cried out, "Mama! Papa! Help me!" At which point I woke up screaming. I remember being terribly shocked, and Heniek and Szymek having to calm me down.

A few times I went back to see Mme Unikowska with whom I had previously lived. She saw how nice and clean I looked and I told her how well I was being treated. I was no longer a skivvy for anybody, particularly not her brat of a daughter. My whole life had suddenly changed for the better. Of course, hunger was still prevalent, but I had pride, a decent appearance and I felt wanted, all of which boosted my morale immensely. I had many new friends and I helped to look after the other children and was part of the general running of things. In this way, everyone learned to help one another.

Among my other friends in the orphanage were two Czechoslovakian boys, Peter and Heinz. Peter was about fifteen years old and had come from Prague, where his father had been a conductor with a Prague orchestra. Heinz, also from Prague, was the son of a lawyer, and had known Peter before coming to the orphanage. Both boys were very intelligent.

The three of us used to walk around the yard of the orphanage, discussing our previous home lives. I learnt much about Czechoslovakia from them. Prague was a very cosmopolitan city, and both boys had come from wealthy families. They were used to having servants and spending money on the things they enjoyed. They had been pampered by their parents, taken on holiday to places such as Sudetenland, Vienna and Budapest. They enlightened me on a life which I never knew had existed.

In Poland the socio-economic life was much lower than that in Czechoslovakia. We were poor, and had never experienced the grandeur that these two boys had been used to. However, although we had never had much in terms of material wealth, we had had a very happy and stable family life.

The life they were now living came as a terrible shock to Peter and Heinz. It went without saying that there was an enormous contrast between Prague and Lodz. They had never seen poverty and starvation, had never been treated as dirt by anyone, and the impact of all this was devastating to them. It was easier for me to come to terms with the situation as I had seen poverty and knew what it was all about.

Our entertainment in the orphanage consisted of occasionally putting on plays, and of holding little concerts for which some of the children would learn and recite poetry. Sometimes we would sing songs, some of which we had learnt in the orphanage and others we had learnt at our schools before the war. On occasions we even had outsiders coming in to perform for us, the most memorable of whom was a man called Mr Perkal, a Polish Jewish writer, who came and gave us some recitations. The one I particularly remember had been written by Tuwima and was about a locomotive. We all sat enraptured by his wonderful performance, watching as he did all the actions of the locomotive such as belching out smoke at the station. It was magical evenings such as this that took our minds off our plight, at least for a short while.

Quieter pursuits in the orphanage included draughts or cards. Some evenings, someone would come and teach us how to draw and paint. As we were forbidden by the Germans to have any schooling, these 'lessons' were done in secret. Like the plays and concerts we put on and the performances we watched, the 'lessons' kept our minds busy, stopped us from thinking about our empty stomachs and the atrocities outside.

A DETAIL OF HISTORY

My room in the orphanage was on the first floor. From the window I could see the people outside the ghetto, and looking down could see the spiked wire fence which separated us from the outside. A German policeman guarded the section of fence that I could see, forever patrolling up and down. On the opposite side of the fence I could see Polish Christian boys playing football and hide-and-seek, enjoying the normal, happy life which I longed for. How I yearned to be free like them, to be able to go into the countryside, breathe fresh air, look at flowers and visit rivers and parks as I used to do with my family. My heart ached with loss when I thought of these things.

One day one of the boys whom I was watching saw me looking at him, and started pulling faces at me and sticking out his tongue. I did the same to him and he laughed. Gradually we began to develop a kind of friendship, silent and distant, using sign language to communicate. This had to be done secretly so that the German policeman would not see us. Every day at the same time I went to the window to see the boy waiting outside; he showed me his toys and even wrote his name - Janek Szczepinski - on a blackboard with a piece of chalk. On occasions he was seen by his father, and was promptly sent into the house, obviously because his father was frightened of the consequences if the German policeman should catch us. This made me very sad, but if we had been caught, the outcome, for me at least, would have been tragic. One day, after Janek had been taken inside and I was standing dejected at the window, Szymek came into the room. He asked me what was wrong, and was horrified when I told him of my secret friendship. "Arek!" he said. "Don't you realise what you are doing? If you are found out you will be in serious trouble!" He took me downstairs and introduced me to his sister, Genia, who had just been accepted

THE ORPHANAGE

into the orphanage. Immediately upon meeting her, I knew that I was in love.

Genia, my first love, made life in the ghetto so much easier to bear. She was a beautiful girl; big brown eyes, black curly hair and a delightful smile. Just seeing her and speaking to her made me feel wonderful. She used to make up stories, write them down and read them to me. Every evening I waited for her to come to supper in the dining room, where we would always sit together and discuss what had happened that day.

Sometimes Genia and I used to walk through the streets of the ghetto. The buildings were drab and overcrowded, the people poor and hungry, and even the trees, of which there were not many, were thin and undernourished. However when I was with Genia my surroundings did not seem to matter. We talked and talked, about our families, our past lives and our hopes for the future.

Genia's parents had owned a clothing shop in Lodz before the war. They had both died of starvation in the Lodz ghetto in 1943. Other members of her family were dispersed throughout Poland. Some of them, she knew, had died in the uprising of the Warsaw ghetto a year earlier.

Whilst in the orphanage, Genia was assigned a job in a leather factory. Sometimes I used to take a circuitous route to work just so that I could walk with her. On the way to the factory we had to pass a bakery, and sometimes we would see men loading up bread for delivery to the other side of the ghetto. The smell which came from the bakery was beautiful, but in our state of ceaseless hunger it was like torture. Nevertheless we used to stand and watch until the bread was all loaded up, yearning for a piece to fill our grumbling stomachs, but knowing that we would not get one. After passing the bakery we turned a corner where we always parted.

A DETAIL OF HISTORY

Genia would say goodbye, then would walk away, leaving me standing there, watching her until she had disappeared into the distance.

Often whilst sitting in the orphanage's large hall in the evenings, we would gather into groups and discuss our future plans. We talked a great deal of our home lives and our families and of our ambitions to resume those lives once the war was over. We would, we all said, seek out whoever remained from our families and settle down to a free, comfortable life with them that was full of happiness and where food and warmth were plentiful. We all had a vague idea of how the war was going; we heard rumours and scraps of news that got through to us. From these rumours it seemed apparent that Germany would soon be defeated, that the day of liberation would soon be at hand.

By June 1944 the rumours of the advancing Russian armies ploughing into the German lines became more and more abundant. It seemed that liberation was getting closer and closer. However, ominously, the slow liquidation of the Lodz ghetto was already underway; each day more and more people were being taken out and transported to unknown destinations. The talk within the ghetto was that they were being sent to Germany to do manual work, primarily in the factories and on the farms in order to supplement the rapidly decreasing German manpower. This trend was disturbing, but I felt sure that Chaim Rumkowski would do his utmost to ensure that we children would be allowed to remain in the ghetto until the bitter end. However in August 1944, when I had been in the orphanage for fifteen months, my dreams were shattered. The order came through that the orphanage was to be closed and that all the children it housed were to leave the ghetto.

Naturally our shared reaction was one of bitter disappointment and renewed fear for our future. We had all thought that it would be simply a matter of time before the Russians liberated us, but we now all realised that this had been merely a pipe dream. Our *kierowniczka* told us to collect our belongings together as we were to be taken away for resettlement. We were told that we must obey all orders that we would be given on our journey. Next morning, 25 August 1944, we all assembled outside the orphanage dressed in what few clothes we had.

There were one hundred and eighty-five of us in all, and we made a pitiful sight; thin, undernourished, frightened and nervous. "Where are the Germans taking us?" was the question everyone was asking, a question to which the *Kierowniczka* could not or would not reply. Some of the younger children were very frightened, and we did our best to comfort them, but in truth there was as much fear in the hearts of us older children too. In particular I think I was more scared than most, as I knew what 'resettlement' meant, and I had seen what the Germans did to children who were too young or too feeble to work.

We set off, carrying the few belongings we possessed. Over my shoulder I had a little blue bag which contained one shirt, one pair of underpants, two handkerchiefs, one pair of socks and a half-finished wooden horse I had been carving. Also in the bag were what I treasured most in the whole world, a number of family photographs. There was one of Tovia and myself standing next to a tree in the park, two of my sisters, Mania and Itka, by the river Warta, three of the whole family with my parents sitting in the middle, two of my grandparents, and a few more of my other family. I looked at the photographs of my parents and thought how much I needed their guidance at that moment. I was fifteen years old, a boy trying to be a man. I knew in my heart of hearts that we were marching to certain death, but I did not say anything for fear of spreading panic, and also through some vain, desperate hope that I might be mistaken.

I saw a boy called Abramek walking in front of me, his face covered in freckles, his red hair like fire in the sunshine. Looking at him, I reflected that we all had tragic stories to tell. Abramek's mother had been ill in one of the ghetto hospitals when in 1942, the SS moved in and cleared all five hospitals out, murdering two thousand of the patients, his mother among them. His father had been caught as a hostage and had to dig his own grave with twenty other hostages before being shot into it by the Germans. I wondered if we were all now about to suffer a similar fate.

We were marched out of the ghetto and towards the railway station, our clogs clattering on the cobbles. Our *kierowniczka* and her husband were at the head of the column, our other teachers walking by the sides. I remember people opening their windows to look at us as we marched past, their faces solemn, and people bowing their heads as we passed them in the street. This reaction confirmed my worst fears and I looked around at all my friends, wondering if they realised as much as I did what 'resettlement' really meant.

The boys walking beside me were my room mates, Heniek and Szymek, and another boy called Beniek. Beniek was twelve years old, intelligent, witty and sensitive. He recited poetry beautifully, was forever cracking jokes and loved music. In the orphanage he had made a piccolo for himself from wood, and used to play it in the concerts we occasionally held in the main hall. Before the war his father had owned a shoe factory.

Due to the starvation diet we had received in the ghetto, we were all very weak and had to stop many times to allow the younger children to catch up. Two other boys, Krol and Motek, began to walk in front of us, and Krol turned back to ask if he could sit with me on the train. He wanted to watch the countryside go by, he said, as before the war he had travelled through the countryside many times by train with his parents on the way to visit his uncle and aunt in Wielun. All Krol's family were now dead; his parents had both died of tuberculosis, and his brother and two sisters had been sent on an earlier transport out of the Lodz ghetto to meet their deaths in Chelmno. I began to talk to the two boys, though little Motek, as usual, was silent. He was thirteen years old, very small and pale, and he had a deformed left hand which meant that he used to stay behind in the orphanage to do different chores while we went off to work.

It was very hot on the march and we were all tired and sweating. All at once the hopelessness of the situation overwhelmed me. I thought, "I am only fifteen years old. I want to be free to go to school and play with other children. I don't want to die yet." I burst into tears, my friends, bewildered, asking me what was wrong. This, to me, showed that they didn't really know what was happening to us. I told them it was nothing, that I was just tired from all the marching, and I dried the tears from my eyes. I thought for the millionth time about my parents, about Tovia and Itka and Mania and our life in Sieradz. To stop the tears from coming again, I focused on four men who were roped together, pulling a truck on rubber wheels that was loaded down with flour. Their bodies were bowed to the ground with the weight of the load, and I thought bitterly, "That is all we are to the Germans, cattle to be worked to death, then slaughtered."

Waiting in the city square were several lorries. My heart began to thump as we were told to stop. Our teachers instructed us to climb into the backs of the lorries, twenty-five children to each one. I made sure I was with Szymek and Heniek. I looked around for Genia, but she was well in front of me, helping with the smaller children at the head of the column.

A DETAIL OF HISTORY

I had a piece of bread hidden in my shirt, left over from my morning ration. On the lorry I was so hungry that I took out the bread and began to eat it, watched by all the other starving children. Unable to contain myself, I ate every last crumb, and afterwards wondered where my next piece of bread would come from. The lorry journey took about half an hour, then the doors were opened and we were ordered out.

We stepped into bright sunshine to discover we had arrived at the railway station. There were people milling about everywhere, being herded into cattle wagons by SS men with guns. The shouts of the guards, "*Schnell! Schnell!*" the grinding of shutters as the cattle wagons were filled up and closed, the frightened cries of little children, the moans of the people, all this was very disturbing.

We were forced to get into line and to shuffle forward as the wagons were filled up. At last our turn came and we were herded into a cattle wagon, packed in like sardines, orphans and strangers alike. The shutters were closed on us, trapping us in humid semi-darkness. 'How will we breathe?' I thought. 'How will we sleep? What will we eat?' There was only a tiny, narrow window at the top of the wagon, no other light or ventilation.

Through the crowd I noticed Genia, together with her brother, Szymek, and Heniek, from whom I had become separated. My heart leaped; at least we would be together, I thought, at least there will be somebody to talk to and care for. I made my way over to them as the train began to move.

As the journey progressed, it gradually grew hotter and hotter in the wagon. Little children began to cry, elderly people began to feel faint, and many people started getting desperate to go to the toilet. I was standing on a bucket, looking out of the tiny window, but had to get down when one of the men asked if he could use the bucket for a makeshift toilet. He fenced off a corner of the wagon with a blanket, then put the bucket behind it. That way people could go behind the blanket and thus retain what little dignity they still had left.

After a while the stench from the bucket became unbearable. However we had to live with it as the doors were locked and the window was too high and narrow to empty out the bucket's contents. The heat, too, continued to build, and little children continued to cry. We could not sit down as the wagon was too cramped, and we were all very hungry. Fortunately a few people had brought bottles of water with them which they began to pass round.

All at once an old woman collapsed, and within minutes was dead. Now, as well as all our other problems, we had a corpse in the wagon with us. I began to pray as never before, "Please God, let us reach our destination soon." My prayers however, went unheeded; the long day dragged on and on, heading slowly towards night.

Eventually one reaches a stage where one resigns oneself to a certain situation. During that long, terrible day I believe I reached that stage for perhaps the first time since the war had begun. I began to care little about my own fate; I just wished that this horrendous ordeal would end, one way or another. Perhaps the only thing that stopped me from giving up completely was the responsibility I felt towards Genia and her brother.

Genia was nervous and trembling with fear. She had never been in a camp before and did not know what to expect. I stroked her face and held her hand, the sweat slippery between our palms. I assured her that we would be all right, that I had been in a camp before and I was still alive. She squeezed my hand tightly, and gradually I was able to calm her down a little.

Every so often I asked Heniek and Szymek to lift me up so that I could look out of the window. When the train curved I could see the guard on the running board outside our wagon, brandishing his machine gun. I wondered how close the Russians really were, whether they would ever release us from this ordeal. Most of all I wondered where this train was taking us.

At last night fell and it began to get cooler, but it also grew steadily darker until it was pitch black. We slept what little we could, half- standing, leaning against one another, but our sleep was punctuated by the smell of sweat and death and human waste, and by the moans and groans of the people. The darkness, like the heat, seemed to go on and on, a night that lasted a year. When, finally, dawn came, it brought very little hope. The train was still speeding on towards its destination, but where that destination was, none of us could say.

We travelled a little further and then, abruptly, the train began to slow down. Once again I asked Szymek and Heniek to lift me up to the window so that I could see what was going on. The sight that met my eyes was what I had been expecting, yet my spirits plummeted all the same. I saw a camp, barracks, high wire fencing, guards in towers, people walking about in striped suits. The train gradually slowed down further and then came to a stop. After a journey that had seemed to go on for ever, we had finally arrived at our destination.

We waited a further ten minutes, then we heard German voices, the noise of the doors being pulled open. Despite our fear, we were urging them to hurry up, to get to our door. All of us were anxious for that precious moment when we would feel sunlight on our faces again and smell the scent of fresh clean air. At last we heard voices outside our wagon, the rattle of the door being unlocked. I smiled nervously at my friends and gathered my few belongings together, ready to disembark.

THE ORPHANAGE

We screwed up our eyes as the brightness of the day hit us, gulped in lungfuls of the wonderful air. However we did not have much time to appreciate it as the Germans began to shout at us, "*Raus! Schnell!*" and started herding us into queues. All around me was commotion. I heard the shouts of the Germans, the screams of lost, frightened children, the cries of mothers frantically searching for their sons and daughters. The SS, the same kind of men who had taken my friends away in those enclosed lorries to their deaths, were very brutal, kicking and beating people into line. There were five thousand people on the platform, which meant there was bound to be some disorder, yet the Germans liked things to be orderly, even when they were taking us to our deaths.

There was a long concrete ramp leading from the station into the camp, along which streamed an endless line of people. We had to wait in a queue for our turn to ascend the ramp, all of us nervous, terrified, trying to keep out of the way of the German soldiers. I saw one young mother screaming and clinging to her children as the SS tried to take them away from her. A number of SS waded in and began to thump and kick her, smashing her nose, knocking her to the ground.

She lay there, screaming horribly with pain, but even then they didn't stop their beating and kicking. I turned away, sickened and shocked, feeling horribly guilty for not going to her aid, but knowing there was nothing I could do, that we simply had to keep quiet and remain unobtrusive, and hope that by some miracle we would survive this nightmare.

Eventually our queue began to move and we were herded towards the long concrete ramp. As we got closer I realised that the Germans were separating people into two rows, one row going to the left, the other to the right. The left-hand row, I saw, was full of children and old people and I knew I had to avoid that one at all costs. As I neared the two high ranking SS officers who were dividing the people into these rows, I drew myself up to my full height and tried to give an impression of strength and fitness.

To my horror the SS men barely glanced at me before indicating that I should join the left-hand row. There was nothing I could do or say; my mind was numb, but racing. I saw that all the children from the orphanage were in this row, shuffling forward, and I joined them, my numbness gradually giving way to an awful sense of terror.

Suddenly behind us a commotion began, perhaps another small attempt at resistance, accompanied by much scuffling and screaming. With the attention of our guards on this commotion, I instinctively stepped across the dividing line into the right-hand row. I merged in with the people in this row, my heart beating fast, my eyes focused downwards on my shoes. I was certain that I must have been spotted, but no guard appeared to tell me to rejoin the children and the old people. I shuffled in through the gates of the camp, still not fully realising what I had done, still not fully aware that I had just saved myself from certain death in the gas chambers. A man in a striped suit working at the side of the road looked up and said very quietly in Yiddish that we were lucky to be in this group. He informed us that we were in Birkenau, Auschwitz, which didn't mean very much to me as I had never heard of the place before.

We carried on walking until we arrived in a small square, surrounded by electric wire fencing and some barracks. We were all men in this group, and we were told to halt and form into rows. We did so, and then simply stood there, waiting for about an hour, facing a door. Suddenly the door opened and a group of women, naked with their heads shaved, ran out, behind them a number of

THE ORPHANAGE

SS men, herding them along with whips. It was obvious from the reactions of many of the men that they were seeing their wives and daughters among this group. I cannot fully explain how degraded and sickened and ashamed I felt at witnessing this awful spectacle. We simply had to stand there and watch as the SS men whipped and beat the women and screamed at them like pigs.

The women were driven out of the square and towards the women's camp. The SS men who were guarding us now began to scream at us, "*Du schweinhunde, schnell, schnell!*" Feeling angry and disgusted, but unable to protest, we were herded into a large hall.

A transport of Jews on the 'ramp' at Birkenau, undergoing selection in May 1944; men in one column, women in the other. The column walking away in the distance is heading towards the gas chamber and Crematorium II. Their belongings, on the far right, will be sorted for German use.

AUSCHWITZ
A matter of survival

In the hall we were told to undress and to leave all our clothes and belongings in front of us. They took away the only photographs I had left of my family, my only link with home, and standing in the large hall I began to weep. Of all the black days during the war, this was undoubtedly, for me, one of the blackest. On this day every one of my friends from the orphanage - Heniek, Szymek, the beautiful Genia, Peter, Heinz - and all but three of the children from the place where I had been so happy, went to their deaths.

We were led from the hall into the showers, and then were taken to another camp in Birkenau known as *Cygainer Lager* - Gypsy Camp - which prior to our arrival had housed four thousand, five hundred gypsies and their families. One day the Germans assembled all the gypsies, gave them food for a journey so as to make them think they were going to a work camp, and had then taken them away in lorries to meet their fate in the gas chambers.

A DETAIL OF HISTORY

The *Cygainer Lager* was a disease-ridden place; we walked around it like lost sheep. The Germans took away every last vestige of human dignity and the food we received was just enough to keep us alive - soup like dirty water. Prisoners were just human skeletons walking around in the compound, some with swollen legs and bodies from lack of fat. During the daily roll calls, which usually lasted for several hours, many of the prisoners collapsed from exhaustion. There wasn't a blade of grass to be seen anywhere as the starving prisoners had eaten it all.

In addition to all this horror we could see the crematorium burning the new arrivals every day; I knew this was so because the *capo* - foreman - had told me what happened to the people who went to the left. Daily we watched clouds of smoke belching out of the chimneys and smelt the awful stench of burning flesh.

That first evening we arrived, about one hundred teenage boys including myself, were gathered together and marched to another barrack. There, numbers were tattooed on our left arm; mine was B7608. This number was our passport to work and maybe our chance to live a little longer.

As we were waiting in the queue, I met another boy from the city of Lodz. His name was Natek, a very pleasant young man. Almost instantly we became very good friends and together with Krol, another of my friends from the orphanage, we decided to stick together. Of all the children in the orphanage, we were the only ones who had survived.

After we had received our tattoos, they cut all our hair off and then they issued us with our concentration camp suits and shoes. I found a good pair of shoes with a Budapest stamp inside, too high and too big, but fine if laced up tightly. The shoes had probably belonged to some unfortunate person who had gone to the gas chambers a few days earlier.

AUSCHWITZ

This procedure over, we were marched back to the Gypsy Camp and into our barracks. Those barracks were horrendously overcrowded with a thousand people packed in at a time. There was very little room to move around, but at least we were alive. The first night was very long; people were moaning and coughing and grinding their teeth in their sleep. My mind was in such a turmoil that I just couldn't sleep. I was thinking about the story that the *capo* had told me about the crematorium. It was unbelievable - and now our barrack was actually overlooking that awful place.

The next day we were awakened very early. We all received a drink of black coffee and a piece of bread. We then had to gather for a roll call, where we had to stand in straight rows to be counted. Afterwards we wandered around aimlessly, until in the afternoon we were given some watery soup in a bowl, but no spoon to eat it with. I had two pieces of turnip at the bottom of my container and to retrieve them I had to use my fingers. 'What food,' I thought. No wonder the people looked thin, pale and malnourished. The Germans in Auschwitz named them *Muselmänner* - literally meaning Muslims, but describing skeleton-like inmates who appeared to have lost the strength to live. These people were often selected for the gas chambers as they were no more use to the Germans.

After two weeks in this camp all the young people in my block were told to report for roll call in order to be chosen to be sent away for work. I was in the second row, and after waiting about ten minutes the SS officer came and started to look up and down the columns of boys. He then started picking out several of them and telling them to wait on the other side. He passed me several times, but didn't choose me, so I decided to stand on my toes to try to be noticed. He passed me once again, then stopped, looked at me, and told me to join the rest of the boys. It had worked. I had survived again and was really proud of myself. Also Natek had got through, as had the other member of our trio, Krol.

After half an hour we were marched off.

We didn't know what camp we were going to, and had been marching for a while when we noticed a brick building in the distance. It had electric wire surrounding it and towers with machine guns. We approached a large gate, above it the sign, '*Arbeit Macht Frei*' - 'Work Makes Freedom.' All at once the noise of a siren split the air and planes began flying above our heads. The SS guards left us and jumped into dugouts at the side of the road. We never moved, we just stood where we were. We had arrived at Auschwitz, the head camp.

Eventually the 'all clear' sounded and the SS men climbed out of their dugouts and led us into the camp. We were taken to a block near the infamous 'Block Eleven' where prisoners were tortured and often executed for minor transgressions of camp rules. I was very apprehensive as we were led through the corridors, half expecting something terrible to be waiting for us around each corner. We were all young boys and were put several to each room - luckily my two friends, Natek and Krol, were in the same room as I was. We waited for half an hour, then I decided to go outside to have a look around.

I saw prisoners who were so thin they could hardly walk, and noticed that everybody was dressed in the familiar striped suits. I went to the back of the block where I saw electric wire fencing, a high wall and every two hundred yards or so, tall watchtowers manned by SS with machine guns.

To me everything seemed so strange. Before the war Auschwitz had been a small town in Silesia, with the river Sola on one side and the river Vistula on the other.

AUSCHWITZ

All the prisoners in Auschwitz were very curious to know how we young boys had 'survived the selection' and not been sent to the gas chambers. We said we thought it was because the Germans were so short of manpower that they were using boys for agriculture, building and ammunition factory work.

The older prisoners did everything possible for us. That first day, as I passed one of the blocks, a *capo* called me in and gave me some bread. Later, towards the evening, I watched the prisoners returning from work, half-dead but made to march in columns like an army. As they passed through the gate there was an orchestra playing, such was the German bestiality.

I was soon to discover there were many smaller 'subcamps' surrounding Auschwitz, including Budy, Plawy, Babice, Harmeze and Monowice. At Monowice, the largest subcamp, later called Auschwitz III, there was the huge Buna Werke (rubber plant) of IG Farben industries. There was a prohibited area of over 15 square miles around the area of Auschwitz. Altogether there were more than forty such subcamps over an even wider area. Most of of them utilised inmates for work in armament-related industry, although some were used for production of food and livestock. There were five gas chambers with crematoria; one at Auschwitz head camp (also called Auschwitz I)and four more at Birkenau (Auschwitz II), the largest of all the camps.

The origin of the gas chambers at Auschwitz had come about following an inspection of the camp by Himmler in March 1941. Shooting and beating was too slow a process, so they had to look for more efficient means of killing. As part of his expansion plans, including the new camp at Birkenau, Himmler requested the construction of large crematoria for incinerating bodies. Later the plans were adapted to assist the extermination of the Jews by adding gas chambers. Hoess, the Commandant of Auschwitz, was instructed to establish Auschwitz and Birkenau as the centre of the extermination programme in the summer of 1941. Birkenau was ideal for them; situated close to the river Vistula it was a desolate place, most of the year damp and misty, and had a railway line close by. It also was hidden by a small forest, which made it the perfect spot for carrying out the plan of mass extermination. The first experimental gassings took place in September 1941 and by early 1942, up to 2,000 Jews each day were being gassed in converted airtight buildings at Birkenau. They used a gas called Zyklon B which had previously only been used to destroy vermin. It was a far more efficient process of mass murder than the vans that had been used at Chelmno from December 1941. After gassing, the bodies were buried in mass graves, and then later, when the graves became too large, they were burned in large trenches. As more and more transports of Jews began arriving at Auschwitz from different parts of Europe, the SS had to build larger installations and by the spring of 1943 had built crematorium I at Auschwitz main camp and Crematoria II, III, IV and V at Birkenau to take the volume of arrivals for extermination. In all, they had the capacity to gas and incinerate nearly 5,000 people each day.

Apart from the hundreds of labour and concentration camps around Europe, there were six death camps in Poland; so called because they were designed with gas chambers for the sole purpose of wiping out the Jews of Europe. Prisoners continued to be killed as well by shooting, beating with sticks and any other form of brutality the guards could devise.

I remember the day our transport arrived at the Birkenau ramp. The wagons were opened and the people were ordered out. The scenes I observed were just too terrifying to imagine. Mothers were

AUSCHWITZ

trying to protect their children as the SS men tried to separate them. The screams of fear from some of the people were appalling to hear. If you were selected to go to the left that meant the gas chambers, whereas to the right meant labour. The choice was entirely that of the SS *Hauptsturmführer* - Captain - Mengele and other doctors. Just before the victims went into the gas chambers, they were told to undress as they were going to have a shower and after that they would be working in the camp. But this was the last journey of their lives.

The average lifespan in Auschwitz was three months, and that only if one was lucky. I had only been in the camp a few days when I had to watch two prisoners (one a Jew, the other a Christian Pole) being hanged. The Pole, who was about twenty-five, was the first, and as they put the noose around his neck, he shouted, "Death to Hitler and the German nation." He was a very brave man, and I suppose he felt he had nothing to lose, but all the same the guards gave him a good beating for his outburst. The Jewish prisoner had to watch this spectacle and then his turn came. I could hear him muttering the *'Shema Yisrael'*. It was a very harrowing experience for me even though I was by now a veteran to violence. I cried with emotion, unable to do anything to help. To witness violent death became a common occurrence. In the morning as I walked out of our block, I could see many prisoners had committed suicide by throwing themselves on the electric wire fence. For some people this was preferable to life in the camp.

The prisoners were easily distinguishable by the different coloured triangles which were worn on their clothing. Jews wore yellow, political prisoners red, Jehovah's Witnesses violet and homosexuals pink. There were different work parties which we used to call *'kommandos'*, a *capo* was a foreman and there were 'over-*capos*' who wore yellow armbands. The trusties on the block wore dark armbands.

Several blocks away from where I was situated was 'Block Ten'. This was where the SS experimented on people, mostly women, who were mainly Jewish. Radiation was used on the genitals of men and women for sterilisation purposes. Many of the young Jewish women had their reproductive organs destroyed by X-ray radiation. As I passed this block a shiver would go through my body at the thought of what the inmates must have been going through. Many other sadistic experiments were carried out on inmates in the name of science and the Nazi ideology. Thousands of prisoners were also killed by an injection of phenol directly into the heart.

The sanitary conditions were dreadful, and resulted in severe dysentery which made made the problems of debilitation and infection even worse. Outbreaks of typhus also killed thousands of prisoners. This disease is transmitted by lice, and as thousands of people slept in each barrack it spread very rapidly. Everyone was weak and undernourished so their resistance was very low, leading to a huge loss of life from epidemics.

At Block Eleven, prisoners were taken for interrogation, but not many came out of the 'bunker' (as it was known) alive. Behind this block there was the 'black wall' where prisoners were shot. A large man called Jacob, a Polish Jew, worked in this block and I met him after the war.

I stayed in the central camp for three weeks and then I was transferred to one of the subcamps, called Budy, which was situated about five kilometres from Auschwitz. On one side of the camp several prefabricated barracks housed the men, on the other side the women. The only time men went into the women's section was for maintenance work. Budy was mainly an agricultural camp.

AUSCHWITZ

Cows, horses and pigs were bred there. I was chosen to look after the horses, feeding and grooming them and cleaning out their stables. Krol and Natek were also chosen to do this kind of work with me. After a while I was told to plough the fields, which was very hard work, following the horses all day long and given very little food to eat.

There was an SS *Hauptsturmführer* - Captain - in charge of our camp who used to enjoy riding his horse, and whenever he rode past me (and other prisoners) he would lash out with his whip for no particular reason other than his own amusement. After several weeks he was sent to the Russian front, which delighted everybody.

We were given sacks of fertilizer to use on the soil. I noticed that mixed in with the powder were small bones, and I was told that it was the ashes of thousands of people who had been burned in the crematoria at Birkenau.

I used to work alongside a Jewish man who always tried to help me and would give me an extra potato whenever he could. I used to wonder why he did it, and then a little later I found out that just two months previously, his own son (who was about my age) had been sent to the gas chamber.

My next job after the horses was to look after the pigs. I would steam potatoes and then mix them with a special feed. This gave me an opportunity now and then to steal a potato when the SS guard was not looking. I remember one day taking a carrot, wiping it quickly on my clothes, and biting into it only to find that I broke a front tooth in doing so. All the produce from breeding livestock and agriculture was for the benefit of the SS and not the prisoners.

I was sent after this to the fishery. In our *kommando* there were five boys amongst the adults: Krol, Natek, Moshe, Yacob and myself. We saw ourselves as a team and stuck very close together.

A DETAIL OF HISTORY

Our job was to go into the river Vistula with nets and catch the fish, which would then be sorted and graded and put into artificial lakes to be caught later when the SS wanted them. On many occasions, when the guard was not looking, we would put a couple of fish into our trousers, and when we got back into the camp would trade our fish for bread from the *capo*. The fishery itself was in a place called Harmeze, which was about three kilometres away from Budy. We would march with our *kommando* there and back each day.

Our life in Auschwitz was a rapid disintegration of mind and body; they dehumanised us completely. Starved and deprived of all human dignity, we quickly became used to the horrors we saw every day. We were reminded daily about going up the chimney, but it soon lost all meaning as we just didn't care any more. The SS did as they wanted with us. To them we were just a flock of animals, filthy lice-ridden slaves. We were so tightly packed in our bunks that when I wanted to get up to go to the toilet I wasn't able to turn, so I just wet the straw that I was lying on. Our bodies were eaten away by filth, infested by lice and we were starved and dying.

Our *capo* in the fishery was Alfred, a German criminal. He was about forty with blond hair, tattooed arms and a very strong body. He had a face like a wild boar, and he would sometimes lash out at some of the prisoners. However he never touched us as we were useful to him; we often smuggled items of food into the camp on his behalf. We all had very high rubber fishing boots that we had to wear, and as I was very small mine used to reach almost to my chest. The work was very hard; we had to wade into the river to catch the fish and more often than not our boots would leak, and, of course, we would get very wet. As autumn was approaching, and it was getting much colder; this for us was ominous.

AUSCHWITZ

Also in charge of us was an SS Second Lieutenant. He was tall, slim and very brutal. He did not like Alfred and was always looking for the smallest excuse to tell him off - and one day he got his chance. As we were sorting out the fish, one of the other prisoners brought in a large bucket containing about fifteen fish and left it with us. Alfred, not knowing that the lieutenant had specially picked these fish out for himself, decided that he was going to have them. He ordered us to smuggle the fish back into the camp for him. I slipped three fish into my trousers, but after several minutes the SS officer returned, looked into the bucket and asked where his fish had gone to. None of us dared to answer. He knew quite well that Alfred had told us to take the fish for himself, but he was waiting for somebody to tell him that this was so. He soon lost patience, and by now the disturbance had created a great deal of interest with all the other SS guards who were watching keenly. He ordered us to take the fish out of our trousers, and we all did as we were told, except that I left one of the fish tucked well down, thinking he would never find it. He still wanted to know who had told us to take the fish, but we dare not betray Alfred, as we were really frightened of what he would do to us if we did. The SS officer ordered us to stand in a row, then walked towards a tree and cut a large branch off.

He called Natek over first and ordered him to bend over, and then proceeded to give him a good hiding until Natek screamed with pain. Next was Moshe, then Krol, then Yacob, and I was last in the queue. All the boys were in terrible pain after their beating, and when my turn came, and I had received the first three lashes, I started running towards the lake which was about twenty yards away. The lieutenant started to chase after me, screaming for me to stop. As I got to the water I suddenly turned right, but he ran straight into the lake and was drenched. By now I was terrified as to what he would do to me, but all he did was call me back and give me several more lashes.

We could hardly walk, the pain was so terrible. About an hour later the same officer told me to sort out some more fish at the table. I bent over, not realising that when he had hit me my trousers must have split and the third fish that I had kept was now sticking out of the hole in the material. He called me over, and I approached him, terrified wondering what he wanted me for. He asked me, "Did you put all the fish back that you took from the bucket?"

"*Jawohl*" - "yes!"

He then told me to take the third fish out of my pants, removed the revolver from his holster and put the weapon to my temple. I began to sweat with fear; I shut my eyes and waited for my death. Icily the lieutenant said, "You took the fish alive, so you will eat it as it is."

A great sigh of relief swept my whole body. Still very scared, I started to tear the fish into pieces and began to eat it along with the blood and the innards. I was feeling very sick, but anything was better than being shot. I carried on eating, and he still had his revolver at my temple, and I thought, 'If I don't eat it all he will shoot me.' Just then a *Sturmbannführer* - Major - pulled up in his horse-drawn cab, and asked the SS officer how things were going. The lieutenant left me, walked over to the major and talked to him for about twenty minutes. This gave me the opportunity to throw the bones and the remainder of the fish into the stream where I was standing.

After the day's work we were marched back to our working camp in Harmeze, where we were called into the Major's office. He asked us who had told us to take the fish from the bucket, but

AUSCHWITZ

still we didn't answer. He kicked me twice in the stomach as I was the nearest to him, and though the pain was unbearable, we still did not dare reveal the truth. The Major had a young Jewish boy working in his office, who said to us, "Why don't you tell him and he will let you go?" After about twenty minutes we were released.

I went back to my small room where I used to repair the rubber fishing boots. As I looked through the window I saw the lieutenant call Alfred over. I saw that the lieutenant had a big stick in his hand with which he started to beat Alfred over the head and body for about half an hour. By the end, Alfred was in a terrible mess, pouring with blood from his wounds. The next day all our bodies were covered in the most shocking bruises and we were in so much pain that none of us were able to work.

We stayed in our block for several days, which was unheard of in Auschwitz. Ordinarily we would have been shot or sent to the gas chambers, but amazingly we got away with it. A few mornings later, the major walked into our block in Budy, and said, "I want to see you all at work tomorrow morning without fail." We obeyed.

I remember many examples of German cruelty. One lunch time I was standing near the wire fence, watching an SS man eating out of his aluminium utensil. He saw me, called me over and asked if I was hungry. I told him I was, so he stretched out his arm as if to give me some food. I reached out receive the food, but before I could touch it he tipped it onto the floor for his Alsatian dog to eat.

In our block we had many nationalities - French, Yugoslav, Polish, Dutch, Greek, and towards the end of the war Italian prisoners of war who refused to fight against the Russians on the Eastern front. One of these Italians, whose name was Mario, came from Rome. All day long he sang 'Mama' and was always talking about his 'beautiful

A DETAIL OF HISTORY

Rome.' He was a born optimist, a dreamer who was forever assuring us that things would work out fine. He was about twenty years old, short, and despite his shaven head had a very pleasant face. I had difficulty communicating with him, as with many of the other foreign prisoners, so we used sign language and gradually Mario and I became good friends. Later, when I was transferred to another camp called Plawy, Mario and I shared a tearful farewell. We hugged each other vowing we would meet up again if we both survived the war. Unfortunately I never saw or heard from Mario again, and to this day I wonder what became of him.

At the height of the extermination of Jews in Auschwitz, there were as many as four and a half thousand people going to their deaths every day. The sky at night was red with the bodies being burned. This job, and the sorting out of the victims' clothes, was done by the 'Sonderkommandos' (special commandos), mainly Jews who were chosen by the SS and numbered about eight hundred. The Sonderkommandos were given better living conditions and had plenty of food to eat as they had to be stronger to cope with so many bodies. Every few months after a major extermination action was completed the workforce was changed; the SS would shoot or gas the last lot and another eight hundred or so would be picked to carry on this task. The reason for this changeover was so that nobody could talk about the factory of death. The men of the Sonderkommando knew that every man who was selected to work in this unit was doomed. The SS guarded them night and day, and any of them that broke discipline was killed.

In the middle of 1944 the Sonderkommando unit was moved into the crematorium compound, where they were completely seperated from the rest of the camp inmates. This had been done for security reasons as the SS quite rightly suspected the

AUSCHWITZ

Sonderkommando were planning an organised uprising. At the same time, they killed one of the Jewish *capos* who was a leader of the resistance and must have been betrayed. However, they still managed to stage a revolt on 7 October 1944. They had hidden a few weapons, and remarkably some explosives had been smuggled through to them from four Jewish women who worked in an ammunition factory. They hoped to get more weapons by killing several SS men. Most of the *kommandos* knew about the breakout and were ready to fight.

The time of the breakout was fixed, but the German *capo*, who was a criminal, surprised a secret meeting of the resistance. As he threatened to betray them to the SS the *kommandos* killed him on the spot and then attacked the SS guards. Due to this, unfortunately the revolt occurred during the day instead of at night, as had been planned. The *kommandos* who worked in Crematorium IV disarmed some of the SS guards, then set fire to the crematorium. It was destroyed by the explosives hidden in the walls.

They then cut some of the wire fences and escaped into the nearby woods. The plan was to receive help from the partisans in the area but unfortunately they were unable to approach the camp during the daylight.

When the *kommandos* of Crematorium II heard the explosion they started a mass escape. In the process they got hold of the over-*capo*, who was a German prisoner, and along with an SS guard threw them both into the furnace alive. They killed another two SS in the breakout, and with some wire cutters they cut the fence that surrounded another camp, hoping to start a mass revolt in the whole of Birkenau camp.

On that day I was working as usual at the fishery. We could hear the sound of sirens, and after a while we saw many SS with their Alsatians, running about, searching the whole of the terrain. They asked our guard if all of us belonged to his work unit and had he seen any prisoners running away. I said to Natek, "There must have been a breakout. I hope they escape." We were ordered to assemble and were all marched back into Budy. All the time, the SS kept a close watch on us, especially as we marched across the fields.

As we went through the camp gates we could sense that something had happened. There was a great deal of commotion amongst the guards on and around the watch towers. I decided to give myself a good wash, but within minutes of my stripping to the waist I was ordered outside for a roll call, much earlier than usual. We had to stand in rows and then we were counted.

They left us standing there for about two hours, by which time we were cold and hungry. Two SS officers ordered us all to get in a crouching position and we were then told to jump up and down like kangaroos. This exercise went on for about an hour and was too difficult for even us boys. The older men simply collapsed, unable to carry on. When the SS officers saw they were not jumping, they lashed out with their whips.

After being outside for about three hours we were told to go back to our block. What a relief. Half dead, everybody dragged themselves inside. Several people had to be carried in with exhaustion.

The breakout was not a success because the *kommandos* ran in a southwesterly direction, towards the Rajsko subcamp, which was still in the Auschwitz zone. They were surrounded and hid in a barn. The SS set fire to the barn and shot the prisoners as they ran out. Twelve men did escape by running northeast and managed to cross the river Vistula, where they hid in an empty building to rest after their ordeal. Eventually, however, the SS patrol, along with their Alsatian dogs, tracked them down.

So ended the unsuccessful escape of the *kommandos* from the Birkenau crematoria; 250 were killed during the uprising and a further 200 inmates of the two crematoria involved in the uprising were shot the same day. But in the process of their revolt they had killed three SS men, and had wounded twelve others. The fact is, they staged it despite utterly impossible circumstances and did hamper the relentless operation of mass murder.

The crematoria continued to work their shifts, but not at the same rate as before, because Crematorium IV had been destroyed.

October soon became November, and the weather grew colder. Our striped suits were very thin, not much use against the Polish winter, and with very little food given to us we were constantly freezing. We couldn't do much outside work as the waters had frozen over, so the SS found us alternative work, and I was given the job of repairing rubber fishing boots.

This job was heaven to me as I was under cover. Every day the SS would deliver the cauldrons of soup for the workers in the camp and they were deposited next to the shed where I worked. After the soup was given out to the prisoners, and whilst the guards had their backs turned, I would sneak out and take some and drink it up as quickly as possible. The soup kept me a bit warmer. The leftovers were taken back to the camp, but I never got a chance to help myself to the fish that was being smoked in the next shed to mine as there was always a guard on duty. The smell was wonderful and it nearly drove me crazy.

On many occasions we would have to go out and set traps for water rats, as the German army used the fur for lining their coats to protect them from the severe winter. Once we caught the rats we killed them, skinned them and then stretched the furs out to dry. Many of the prisoners used to take the rats back to the camp to cook because they were so hungry.

As the winter progressed I got terrible frost bite on my hands and feet. Wounds opened up and I was in a shocking state. I could not go to the medical man because I was in fear of my number going into the register which would have resulted in my being selected to be killed, so instead I managed to get some paraffin from one of the other prisoners, and rubbed it into the affected areas to get some relief.

December 1944, and Christmas was approaching. We were getting news through from the partisans that the German armies were getting a good hammering on all fronts. We knew it wouldn't be long before the war came to an end, and we had no alternative but to be patient. We heard that the Red Army was not too far away, which meant that we might soon be liberated.

In the meantime life continued as normal: out at six in the morning with a cup of black coffee and a piece of bread to sustain us for many hours in sub-zero temperatures.

Our block *capo* was German. He wasn't a bad fellow and whenever possible he tried to help our group of boys. On Christmas Eve our SS sergeant, who was Austrian, walked into our block. His jacket was undone, he wore no hat, and he was obviously very drunk. He shouted "Merry Christmas," and started singing '*Stille Nacht*' - Silent Night - waving his arms about, encouraging us to join in. We simply stared at him silently. Two days later he beat one of the prisoners almost to death for no reason, which underlines the mentality of the SS men.

On 6 January, 1945, our group from the fishing *kommando* was transferred to a subcamp called Plawy, another agricultural camp

AUSCHWITZ

similar to Budy (this is when Mario and I shared our emotional goodbye). We were in Plawy for just twelve days when, on 18 January, we were started on what would be a death march towards Germany. At that particular time there were about forty-two thousand men and eighteen thousand women in Auschwitz camp. There was no rail transport available as it was needed for the retreating German armies, and so thousands of prisoners had to start marching towards Germany, guarded by SS men and with hardly any rations.

Auschwitz camp was liberated on 27 January, 1945, just nine days after we were taken on our march to Germany. The first army to enter Auschwitz was the Soviet Sixtieth, commanded by Marshal Koniev.

Prisoners on a death march.

MARCH OF DEATH
Evacuation to Buchenwald

One day, when almost everyone else had gone out to work, I was ordered to stay behind and clean our cell block. The other prisoners and I were sweeping the floor when in walked the Camp Commandant, Richard Baer, and a uniformed woman. This woman, who carried a whip in her hand, I recognised as Maria Mandl, the Commandant of the women's camp. We had all heard of her and of her extremely brutal behaviour.

The three of us stopped sweeping and stood still. My heart pounded with nervousness. It was not usual for prisoners to be accosted by high-ranking SS officers face to face; usually, if we saw people of such rank, they were accompanied by a number of other SS officers. We had, however, begun to expect changes recently. We all knew that the Russian armies were now not far away. On days when we went outside the camp to work, we saw columns of the German army in retreat; we saw guns and horse-drawn artillery.

A DETAIL OF HISTORY

The German soldiers now looked dejected and not triumphant. Some, I had seen, were only about fifteen years old, no older than I was. We had, in addition to making our own observations, received information from the Polish partisans, who told us that any day now there was a possibility of our being liberated by the advancing Russian army. We just needed to last out a few days longer. Nevertheless, for the moment we were still prisoners of the Germans, and still at their mercy.

Richard Baer stepped in front of me. He looked at me and said in what was meant to be a pleasant tone, "Do you find the food good here?"

I was suffering from starvation, but yet I said, "*Jawohl*." I dared not say anything else. He looked at Maria Mandl and they both seemed pleased by my answer.

"We are going to let you have some film shows," he said.

I nodded to let him know that I thought this would be a treat. Privately I thought, 'Pigs might fly.'

For about ten minutes he and Maria Mandl walked up and down the cell block, addressing the odd word to each other. Then they left. We tried to continue sweeping, but the shock of their visit left us almost paralysed with fright. It seemed to me that the visit was as good an indication as any that Germany was defeated.

Later that day my friend Natek returned from work, bringing with him a bag of semolina which he had taken whilst the SS men were cleaning a food warehouse. There were probably two kilos of semolina in this bag, and later we were to appreciate it greatly as it turned out to be our only food for days.

The day after the visit of Baer and Mandl we were told to assemble outside our block. With a few SS men guarding us, we started to march off. We did not know where we were going, but it was certainly not to the film show we had been promised.

MARCH OF DEATH

The month was January, it was bitterly cold, everything was frozen. We marched in our thin striped suits; we had no coats and no provisions. I had on my Dutch clogs, but no socks, and the wood chafed against my skin and bones. Before we left, I said to Natek, "Whatever you do, don't leave that bag of semolina behind." I made sure he carried it with him.

This was a very severe winter. We had no way of keeping warm except to continue moving. At about three o'clock in the afternoon, when it was already getting dark, we heard the noise of heavy guns. 'It won't be long now,' I thought.

Someone said that maybe the Russians would encircle us as we marched, and the guards began to try to speed us up as they were becoming afraid. They would probably have preferred to run off and save their own skins. As we looked back, we saw that the sky was as red as fire. Some prisoners began to falter, malnutrition and exhaustion preventing them from maintaining the pace the guards demanded. Some asked the guards if they could rest for a while, but the guards just pushed them on. Those who could not walk any more were shot in the back of the head by an SS guard who marched at the rear of the column.

I plodded on. I was almost falling from exhaustion, but knew there was to be no respite. At both sides of the road people lay dead, shot for not being able to walk any further, murdered when they were so close to liberation. Those of us who could, kept on walking. We did not know where we were marching to, only that we were leaving Auschwitz behind.

The guards began to push us more and more. Through half-closed eyes, I was still able to watch the German army on the retreat, and this sight spurred me on. I was aware that this was not the mighty German army which I, as a ten-year-old boy, had watched marching into Poland; this defeated rabble was simply struggling to hold out.

As we marched, we heard an aeroplane approaching. It fired a rocket, which lit up the whole terrain. Bombs fell on a factory close by. In spite of the danger to us, we were exhilarated by this.

We went on marching. I became more and more tired, and began to think that if we didn't stop soon I would simply fall asleep in the road. It was now about four o'clock in the morning, and the guards were tired too. This made them less patient and much more dangerous. I tramped on, not daring to stop even for a second. I had seen what happened to people who did stop. "I am not going to be one of the dead," I promised myself.

Eventually we began to approach a small town. Suddenly we were ordered to stop. We were directed into an empty school where we were told we would be resting for a few hours.

We had been on this march for about twelve hours. Many of those who had started out had been shot for falling by the wayside. The rest of us were half-dead with fatigue and yet we rushed in. We collapsed on the floor with exhaustion and relief. We were given no food. Natek and I ate some of the semolina, digging into the bag with our fingers. This kept us going.

After three hours, during which we slept or simply lay there unmoving, we were ordered to march again. My right foot began to hurt where the back of the clog had rubbed my heel, tearing the skin away, and I had nothing to cover it with. It grew more and more painful, but there was nothing I could do. To complain to the guard invited a bullet through my head. I was forced to march on, further and further, for another day and another night. The pain became unbearable; my foot bled and bled. However, I could not give in.

MARCH OF DEATH

More and more prisoners were being shot and their bodies kicked onto the roadside. As we marched, I prayed that the SS guards, escorting us on both sides of the column, would desert and leave us to the advancing Russian army.

Those of us who were left continued to move on. Deep snow covered the ground, and the frost and wind in the unsheltered countryside lashed at our frail bodies. The thin striped Auschwitz uniforms gave us little protection in the freezing temperature.

On the ground as we passed we saw more bodies, together with pots, clogs and other articles abandoned by prisoners who had gone before us and were too weak to retrieve them.

We had not the energy to talk to each other. We were just walking skeletons. Many gave up, unable to walk any further. We heard many shots. Each shot told us that another exhausted, starved prisoner had got a bullet in the back of the head. It was important to the SS that no one was left behind who would be able to tell about Auschwitz and the horrors which had been perpetrated there.

We received no food at all on the march. The cold became more and more severe. Our column moved on and on along the road. More bodies were strewn in the ditches.

Once again, nightfall, and we were told to stop. This time we stopped in the open. Some of us just sat there in the snow to catch a few moments of sleep, the wind biting into our skins. The open fields gave us no shelter, simply increasing our suffering. I found that my mind was no longer working. I could no longer think. I fell asleep.

We were awakened by shouts from the guards: *"Schnell, schnell!"* Dazed, we stumbled to our feet and moved on, passing several villages. I had it in mind to make a run for it, but with my striped clothing and my shaven head I knew I would not get far.

A DETAIL OF HISTORY

Yet several prisoners did manage to escape from the columns. We heard later that they had been liberated by the Russian army on the advance.

Eventually, we reached a large town, Katowice. There we were marched to the railway sidings and put onto goods wagons. The journey on these wagons, destination unknown, lasted for several days, during which time we were still given no food by the Germans. Natek and I staved off hunger and were probably kept alive by eating the rest of the semolina.

Eventually we arrived at our destination: Buchenwald, a camp in Central Germany. My foot was now in a terrible condition and I hoped some food might be given to me. We were unloaded like cattle, frozen, half dead, desperate for food. Somehow we had enough spirit in us to feel humiliated by this treatment. Perhaps surprisingly, we welcomed the thought of being put in another camp; at least if we were there, there was hope of food and drink.

We were immediately taken into a building to be deloused. Inside the building were several SS men who told us to put our clothing on one side and then to go through a shower. The feeling of the hot water on our bodies was unimaginably comforting. After this we were made to pass two SS men who pumped disinfectant powder under our arms and on our genitals in order to kill the lice with which we were all infested. After this treatment we were marched off, so many at a time.

My column was taken to a block which was half-filled with Russian prisoners of war. Natek and I stuck together like Siamese twins. We were now all each other had.

The block was a large prefabricated building. In it we were directed into bunks, wooden boxes filled with straw. We were crowded together, packed in like sardines, but at least we were under cover and clean. I lay down on my bunk to ease my throbbing, infected foot and saw a young man of about twenty facing me. He wore a Russian army uniform, though with no belt or insignia.

He began to talk to me in Russian, which I understood well enough. He told me that his name was Misha and that he came from Smolensk in Russia. He had been taken prisoner by the Germans whilst serving in the Russian army. He smiled and said that I looked exactly like his younger brother, Sergei.

In the time I was in the camp, Misha and I became very friendly, talking of our homes and our families and the things that had happened to us. He asked one of the Russian prisoners, a medical man, to get me something for my foot, and I was brought some white powder. I put this on my heel, and soon, as if by some miracle, it began to get better.

And so began life in Buchenwald. Terrible as it was, at least we had shelter, a small amount of food and the opportunity to sleep some of the time.

Much of what I saw in Buchenwald was similar to Auschwitz. Every day we watched men with little pushcarts carrying out dead bodies from the blocks and taking them to the crematorium. The bodies were piled ten to a cart and were generally little more than skeletons. We had more roll calls and were given a little food - watery soup, and bread which was weighed by Itzchak, a young boy who had made a scale from the lids of shoe polish tins with some string and a piece of wood. He weighed the bread because we had to share it between six people and each crumb was like gold.

We received more punishments. Sometimes we had to stand for two hours or more to be counted when something did not please the guards. One day I was told that Leon Blum, the Jewish ex-Prime Minister of France, was in the camp. I did not see him personally, but the news, which filtered through via special committees set up in Buchenwald and linked to the outside, was generally reliable.

Likewise, these same committees brought news through of more and more Allied armies advancing towards our part of Germany. 'Surely it won't be long now,' we thought. 'Where else can the Germans send us?' Yet every day people were selected and sent to different parts of Germany, my friend Misha being one of them. When he left I was very sad, as I knew I would never see him again.

One day our *capo* told us that we were being transferred to Block Sixty-six. That was the block that housed a lot of boys and everybody in the camp tried to ensure that we were treated a little better. Our *capo*, called Gustav, was a Czechoslovakian Jew and he was marvellous to us. On certain occasions we got more soup, and on Sundays, as a special treat, we received three potatoes extra. Many times as I was peeling my potatoes, some of the Hungarian Jewish prisoners held their hands underneath to catch the peel and eat it, they were so hungry. They were not yet used to the hunger as they had only been in the camps for about a year. We Polish Jews had had five years to get used to the starvation, the degradation and being treated like subhumans.

Buchenwald was situated in Central Germany near Weimar. It was also near Jena and Erfurt. I remember one night there was a bombing raid on Erfurt, as it was an industrial town. The planes had to come down low over our camp to get to their targets, and the weight of the bombers passing overhead made the whole barracks sway. When the bombs exploded, they made, to me, a lovely sound. I was hoping that the planes would bomb more and more. Our camp was lit up by the flashes of rockets as the planes passed.

MARCH OF DEATH

It was now February, 1945. It couldn't be long now, we thought, as we had heard the American Army was not far away. Sometimes I walked to the main gates of the camp to watch the Ukranian SS units. I was very scared of them, even more so than the German SS, as the Ukranians were even more barbaric. Because of this, I have always since kept away from Ukranian people. They have always been noted for being very antisemitic, and though I realise they are not all alike, I am still very apprehensive of the older ones. By now we were hearing of many places being liberated, and thinking how lucky they were to be free. With the rumours spreading like wildfire that the American tanks were not far away, we thought that we would surely be next. We talked about where we might go. Some of us hoped that we would one day reach Palestine, the promised land.

I watched the distant horizon, buoyed up by the thought that one day I would see the first American tanks appearing over it. It was now the end of March, but we had no romantic thoughts of spring. Its coming simply indicated that the terrible winter was over and that it would now get warmer. We saw more and more planes overhead; the squadrons which passed were growing bigger. Looking up, we could see the American star on the fuselages of the planes.

April arrived. One day, as I was walking towards Block Sixty-six, I saw a great deal of activity. People were talking in excited groups, saying that the Germans had decided to evacuate Buchenwald. If this were true, it was terrible news.

"It can't happen," I said to Natek. "It can't be true, not now."

My fellow prisoners all felt the same way. They talked of the American tanks which could not be more than twenty kilometres away. Some people assured us that there was no need to worry; the Americans would liberate us before the SS had time to get us all out of the barracks.

A DETAIL OF HISTORY

I entered our block and saw that some of my friends were gathering their few belongings together. I could not believe that this was happening. At last two hundred armed SS men came into the camp to clear us out. We were ordered to assemble, and four thousand, five hundred of us were taken out. I was one of them, Natek was another. As we marched towards the main gate, I said to Natek, "We must try to do something. If only we can get away." Natek did not reply, he just shrugged his shoulders.

We were on the march again. It was now 7 April, 1945. I began to wonder how much longer I could survive, and whether my luck had finally run out.

Those who remained alive at the end of our month-long train journey were photographed at the point of liberation by a Czech partisan.

TO THERESIENSTADT
The train of damnation

As we marched off in columns in the late afternoon, I looked around, noticing how beautiful the fields and the forests were. I watched the birds flying free, and I thought, 'Everything is free, except us.' I began to ask myself what our fate was to be. I complained to the silent Natek that we had been so near to freedom several times, and each time it had been snatched away from us at the last minute.

We continued and saw a city in the distance. I thought, 'This must be Weimar.' On this march my problems were increased by the fact that an SS man with an Alsatian kept close to my side. I had always been apprehensive about Alsatians, as I had once been bitten by one at the instigation of an SS guard. Walking, already painful, was made more difficult by the need to keep a distance between me and this beast.

At last we reached Weimar. We were marched towards the railway sidings and loaded on to open goods wagons. We were crammed in like sardines, about one hundred and twenty people per wagon, so that we couldn't even sit down. It was April, which meant the weather was turning wet and windy, and here we were at the mercy of the heavens with no coats or covers.

In all, the transport had four thousand, five hundred people. All of Block Sixty-six were loaded together, so all the boys were on the same wagon. Several brought blankets with them from the camp, but we were still cold, wet and cramped.

Evening approached and it grew much colder. We were given neither food nor drink. The SS guards shut all the doors, the locomotive began belching out steam and we started to move. At last we were on our way to our next destination, though God only knew where that would be.

The night was long and we spent it standing up, half asleep. Standing together helped keep us a little warmer. The train sped on, further and further from Buchenwald. We all wondered what our fate would be. Liberation, which had been in all our minds, now seemed far away again. I was tired, hungry, cold and miserable; I felt half-dead. I was only fifteen years old, but I had seen some of the worst horrors man had ever perpetrated against man.

Dawn came. The sun rose slowly. Everything was damp with dew and we were all feeling tired from standing up all night. The train started to slow down, but I couldn't see what was going on because I couldn't reach to pull myself on to the top of the wagon. As the train came to a halt the SS men began shouting. Our door was opened and I saw that there weren't any houses in sight, just fields and a stream nearby. We were told to have a drink of water from the stream and a wash. We went to the side of the field to urinate because there was nothing in the wagon, not even a bucket. We were all very hungry as we hadn't had any food since Buchenwald, eighteen hours earlier.

TO THERESIENSTADT

I searched about on the ground, hoping to find some corn seeds to eat, but before I could find anything the guards began to shout, "*Schnell, schnell!*" and ordered us back on the wagon. I looked around at the guards, noting that many were Ukrainian SS men, the most savage of all. Others included middle-aged Hungarians, the younger ones having been sent to the front line to fight. I kept my distance from the Ukrainians; they frightened me greatly.

The train started to move again. Looking up, we saw some American fighter planes which swooped low over our heads a number of times and then disappeared. Our spirits rose; they must have known we were prisoners by our camp clothing. Onwards the train sped, hour after hour, another night rapidly approaching. Still we were given no food and once again we were exposed to the freezing night air. When would all this ever end? That night some men died through lack of food.

A wagon a little further down had been reserved especially for the dead. As our bodies were nothing but bones from malnutrition, the wagon soon filled up. Every day we watched as more and more bodies were thrown into the wagon, and when the train stopped at a quiet place they buried the bodies to make room for more. On the third afternoon we were all given a piece of bread - what joy - and a cup of black coffee as a bonus.

We passed towns and villages where everything was so green and healthy, saw people walking freely, well-fed cows and horses grazing in the fields. How picturesque it all looked, how glittering the rivers and lush the forests. It provided a stark contrast to our own situation - packed into a railway wagon, dying a slow death.

I made a large hole in the side of the wagon with a knife so that I could look out and see where we were going. Once again the train came to a stop and everybody was ordered out. I saw two houses half a kilometre away. I said to Natek and another boy with whom we had become friendly, called Yacob, "Wouldn't it be marvellous if we could make a run for it and hide until the train has left?" It was a tempting thought, but we would never have made it. We had no papers and the roads were full of Hitler Youth and police.

We ran into the fields to urinate, but the SS men kept a very close watch on us. They allowed us out for two hours. I decided to pick some grass and get some twigs to make a fire and try to cook it. After about ten minutes I had a good fire going, which I surrounded with stones. My friend Yacob and I started cooking the grass, but we had to keep a good eye out in case somebody tried to grab it from us. This is what hunger had reduced us to.

After eating the grass we found we couldn't digest it; it just sat in our stomachs. It gave us both stomach ache, but at least we didn't feel hungry any more. Soon the guards were shouting, "*Schnell! Raus!*" and ordered us back on the train. We hadn't even been able to have a proper wash because there had been no facilities.

I looked around me and saw lice crawling all over people's bodies. I was no different, I was alive with lice myself. Some people were absolutely covered from head to foot in these creatures. Lice formed just one of the many horrors we suffered, though in some ways it was the worst.

We were now able to sit down at night as several older people in our wagon had been transferred elsewhere. Each night more people died. The dew was slowly getting worse, and every morning we were wet through, cold and hungry.

One morning we stopped at a small station. I hoped the SS would bring us food as I was so hungry. As soon as they let us off the train, I ran to get more grass to eat, but about half an hour later

TO THERESIENSTADT

the Germans brought us some bread. I put my finger down my throat and vomited the grass up, then ate the bread ravenously. We stayed on that particular station for a few hours.

As night fell we all had to climb back onto the wagon and stand all night. About midnight we heard the sound of guards walking outside, then our wagon door was pulled open and we were all told to climb down. We saw to our delight large containers with soup. We were all given some and like hungry vultures we devoured it quickly.

The soup, however, was horribly salty. It was so bad that it burned our stomachs, and the SS would give us no water to quench our terrible thirst. The train started moving again, and next morning we stopped near a river. As soon as we were let off the train, we raced down to the river to drink. The water was not very clean, but who cared? In our condition it tasted wonderful.

As we were drinking, SS guards began, without warning, to open fire on us. In all they killed ten people. We never received any explanation for this sudden, murderous action. Most likely the guards were just bored and had shot at us for sport.

Back we climbed onto the train and the nightmare journey continued. People were dying with more frequency now, their bodies, little more than skeletons, being thrown out of the wagon. I felt anguish for them, thinking, 'If only they could have lasted out a little longer, they would have been free.' I heard a noise in the sky, engines roaring overhead, and looking up I saw the sky slowly filling with bombers. Everything seemed to tremble on the ground from the sound of the planes.

Soon the anti-aircraft guns opened up and started firing in all directions. We all knew that the bombers had not come just to rescue us, but the spectacle was uplifting nevertheless. As we watched, we saw smoke start to pour from one of the planes which had obviously been hit. Slowly the bomber separated itself from the rest of the formation and started to spiral down, engulfed by fire. Suddenly the plane exploded and fell towards the ground. The crew had died, but at least they had fought as free men.

One day one of our men brought the news that Buchenwald had been liberated by the Americans on Wednesday, 11 April, 1945. This was only nine days after we had been marched out. We had been the last transport to leave. It was as if a knife had been put through our hearts. All the people who had stayed behind had been liberated. We spoke in terms of dejection at this cruel piece of luck. It was difficult, after such a twist of fate, to go on hoping. I looked around at the boys in our wagon. We were now all so thin there seemed to be no life in us. I wondered then if any of us would last out. I thought, 'But who knows what will happen next? We have nothing to lose. Hope is the only thing we have left.'

Again the train stopped and again we were let out. All too soon, however, the guards were shouting to us to get back on board once more. We had now been travelling for ten days, but each day seemed like a year. After a while it started to rain. It was only light, but even so we were soon drenched. We were open to all weathers, nothing to cover ourselves with, exposed and vulnerable, cold and hungry.

I looked up at the sky. There had been little opportunity for prayer or the practice of any faith since the time I had left the Lodz Ghetto. Now, however, I did find myself talking to God. I said, "If you are up there in Heaven, why don't you help us?" I found myself asking God to tell me what crime I had committed in my life for which I was being punished. I was still not sixteen years old when I asked God this.

TO THERESIENSTADT

"I have suffered more than most people of ninety," I protested to him. "And my only sin is being born of Jewish parents." It is likely that my parents would have disapproved of my speaking to God in this way, but I was desperate and dejected. I sat in the corner of the wagon and wept.

Once again the train started to move. It was now 17 April, 1945. After travelling for several miserable hours, we stopped. This was a relief as my poor bones were twisted and tossed by the motion of the train. Yacob, seeing my misery had not abated, called over to me, "Arek, come over here and sit under the blanket. It will be warmer for you." I did as he said. I was wet and cold, but huddled up to him, trying to keep warm. I felt a little comforted. Everyone tried to find warmth and comfort from the bodies of others in this way.

I noticed that our Hungarian guard, a man of about fifty-five, was beginning to feel the strain. He began to shiver and moan to himself. He had been exposed to the open as we had, but he had had plenty to eat. We had watched as he drank Schnapps and ate salami with bread. Also he had a long army coat and blankets. And yet the moaning went on.

The train pushed on. By now it was midnight. I was too wet and too hungry to sleep. Fantastic thoughts came into my mind. I thought that maybe I should try to escape the very next time the train stopped. I fancied myself running until I came to some remote farm. I would get a job on this farm, telling the farmer I would do anything so long as I could have food. I persuaded myself that the German farmer would not hand me over to the police. He would not desist from doing this out of kindness, but because he would reason that the war would finish any day now and that evidence that he had treated a poor Jewish orphan with kindness would be to his advantage. Such thoughts as this came into my mind. I stood up in the train, resolving that I must do some such thing before it was too late. All this time the Hungarian guard moaned, his gun in his hand, his eyes half-closed.

Escape was not possible. "What is the use of thinking such things?" I asked myself angrily. I answered myself, "It was just a thought."

The desire to know how far away the Allied armies were consumed us. However, nobody knew this. And nobody dared ask the guards for fear of being shot on the spot.

Dawn broke. We were travelling very fast. The sun came up, and we hoped that it would be warm enough to dry us after last night's rain. Most of the boys stood up to stretch their limbs and to try and dry themselves in the sun.

Everybody looked so dirty, dejected and hungry and they were all scratching themselves from the lice. Some of the prisoners had camp hats, others had none, but we all had our heads shaved. The train slowed down while we were passing a small station and then we came to a stop. After several minutes the SS guards told us to disembark. We had stopped at the perimeter of the station, but with the train being very long we could walk the length of it. It was now a quarter past eleven in the morning according to the station clock. Yacob and I went to get some grass and water so that we could at least fill our stomachs. We made a fire with some paper and twigs and put our little pan on top. I was just putting some more twigs on the fire when suddenly we heard the roar of engines from all sides.

We looked up and saw fighter planes with American markings. They began to strafe everything that was on the station. I shouted to Yacob to take cover, and then we both made a dash and threw

TO THERESIENSTADT

ourselves into the first ditch we could find. Two of our guards were only a few feet away from us, but they ignored us; they were more terrified than we were.

Another swoop and then the planes stopped firing. They flew so low they must have noticed our striped clothing. As they flew away, we dashed back to our pan to find that it had been hit by one of the bullets when the planes had strafed us. We were horrified: if we had stopped where we were, we would probably have been killed.

The destruction of our pan meant that our meals had now gone. Furthermore it meant we had nothing in which to collect rainwater to drink. So what did we do now? I decided to look on the ground for corn or wheat grain, knowing that on many stations they loaded grain on to goods trains. To my joy I found some. They were full of sand, but I wiped them on my clothes and ate them; anything to keep alive. When I walked back to my wagon I saw that more bodies were being thrown on, and I thought to myself, 'Anything is better than this.' I was given some high leather boots when I was in Buchenwald camp and I now decided to burn pieces of leather from the top and chew it. My boots gradually became shorter and shorter as time went on.

We passed a number of big cities; Chemnitz, Andberg, Bucholtz, Jachymov. 'Where on earth are they taking us?' we thought. At times we were going forward, and then back to previous destinations, most likely to avoid the advancing Allied armies liberating us. We had now been travelling for eighteen days and were feeling more dead than alive. The transport was getting smaller as more and more people died. I was slowly beginning to lose hope.

It started to rain again. I thought 'I might as well sit back and wait for my death.' I was getting drenched, my clothes sticking to my body. I asked Natek if I could get under his blanket to share a little warmth. He agreed readily, and together with Yacob, the three of us sat and shivered and sneezed with the cold. The blanket gradually grew heavier and heavier with rain.

Night fell, the rain got lighter and then finally stopped. The train was travelling at a very high speed. I fell asleep and when I woke we were on the outskirts of Karlsbad.

Soon the train was stopping again, and after a while the SS guards ordered us off the wagons. My clothes were still soaked; I was freezing cold and itching like mad from the lice. Walking along the platform, I noticed somebody had brought us bread and black coffee. We stood in a queue to receive our share. At least it would warm us up a little, I thought.

After the food and drink I went for a walk, just down the length of the train, to stretch my legs, rubbing my cold hands as I did so. Arriving back at my wagon, I stopped to talk to a friend of mine from Vilna, who was called Maier. Preoccupied, we both climbed onto the wagon, myself not realising that my hand was in the door. Suddenly someone slammed the door on my fingers. Oh, the agony! My hand had been scraped free of skin and there was no medical help. I didn't know what to do. In the end I urinated on the wound as someone told me it acted as a disinfectant. With everybody back on the train, we began moving again, the engine belching out steam. The sun started to get warmer and my clothes began to dry a little. The train picked up speed.

I was sitting near the old Hungarian SS guard. He murmured something about Hitler, but I couldn't hear properly because of the noise of the train. Ten minutes later he said to me, "It won't be long. You will soon be free." I looked at him with bewilderment, not believing what he was saying.

TO THERESIENSTADT

He told me Hitler was dead. Somehow I knew he wasn't lying to me. I never told anybody until we stopped at the next station, and then I told some of the boys and the news spread like wild fire. If Hitler was dead, the German army would not fight on and the war would soon be at an end.

Thank God. We had made it. We came to a station called Neesse (Egar). On the other line some women from another camp were being transported elsewhere, but they didn't know where to. I climbed up onto one of the wagons and looked in. Before my eyes was a whole wagon full of dead bodies, all women, all unclothed, just skeletons. I was sickened by the sight. I jumped down and walked back to my own train. Maier said to me, "Have you heard what the SS are going to do?"

I looked at him in surprise. "No, tell me," I replied. He informed me that all the boys from our wagon were going to be put in a row in front of the train and ordered to drop their trousers, and those who were circumcised (meaning the Jewish boys) would be taken away and shot. My heart started pounding. "Oh God, what can we do now??!" I said.

A terrible dilemma faced us; either stay and be shot, or make a run for it and be shot. I climbed onto the train and saw Itzhak and two brothers called Haim and Jankl. I told the three of them that we had nothing to lose and suggested we make a run for it. I told them that over on the other side was an empty goods train and we could hide in one of the wagons. They agreed and we prepared to make our escape.

We were very quiet as we went about it; if the SS men had seen us we would have been shot on the spot. We waited in there for about an hour, looking out through a crack in the wagon, watching all the boys milling around. Our hearts were pounding in fear of discovery. Each minute we expected the shooting of Jewish boys to begin, but nothing happened, and eventually we decided to return to our transport and take our chances with the rest. Half an hour later we were ordered back on the train. It seemed the rumour had been wrong, after all.

We started off again on the journey that seemed to have no end. Overhead some fighter planes swooped down over the train, but they didn't fire on us. The pain in my hand was now unbearable, and I had nothing to put on to relieve it. I spent much of the time looking out through a crack in the wagon wall and reading the names of the stations we were passing through. Several of them now had Czech-sounding names. The train started to slow down and came into a station called Marienbad. We were ordered off and given some bread. It now seemed we really were in Czechoslovakia.

I looked over at the other side of the station, saw people walking about, talking to each other. I thought, 'Aren't they lucky to be free?' It was now 29 April, 1945. Hitler was dead and yet nothing in our lives had altered. Soon the guards were shouting at us to get back onto the train and the doors were slammed shut. I noticed an army transport pass by with several artillery pieces and some shire-horses in the enclosed wagons.

After several minutes we were on the move again, and a little later we came to a place called Rakovnik. Then it was on to Zatek, where we stopped and were told to disembark. There was some water for us to drink and I also managed to have a wash. I was very hungry and the pain in my finger was getting much worse; in fact it had turned septic and by now I was in agony. I started to cry with pain, and through my tears saw Maier walking towards me holding his shoulder. I asked him what was the matter, and he told me that one of the SS men had shot at somebody and he had accidentally got the bullet in his shoulder. It was very painful for him, but, like me, he had to endure his pain. There were no medical supplies and we didn't know what to do. The SS began to scream, "*Schnell! Schnell!* Get back on the train!" Soon we started our journey again.

The train then passed through a town called Louny, but it did not stop. In fact it seemed to pick up speed and began racing faster and faster and faster. I looked up at the overcast sky, dreaming and hoping for release.

After some time we came to a railway station in a place called Roundnice. After about ten minutes we were ordered to get off the train. I saw that on the platform were several Czechoslovakian policemen, young fellows who came over to talk to us and ask us where we had come from. They saw our starved bodies and the horror of our conditions on the train, and seemed unable to believe that such a thing could be happening. Some of them wept in front of us. We stood and watched them silently. They asked us if we would like some food, and we begged them to give us some. One of the policemen went away to get it.

When he returned we did not snatch it from him, but just held out our hands. I saw that on the other side of the transport another policeman was giving boys some bread and meat. One of the Ukrainian SS guards also saw this, and he turned his rifle round to get hold of the barrel to hit one of the starving boys over the head. A Czech policeman saw what was happening and drew his revolver. He pointed it at the SS guard and said, "If you touch this child, I will shoot you." I saw the SS guard immediately put his rifle down and walk away. We realised that something we had never seen before was happening: an SS guard had taken orders from someone else.

Soon after that the Czech policemen rounded up all the SS guards and took them away. It was said later that they had shot them.

A DETAIL OF HISTORY

Our train was slowly taken into Theresienstadt. This happened on 4 May, 1945.

Theresienstadt had brick-built buildings, very much a fortress town. There were no SS guards about when our train pulled in, and we were told to disembark and were taken to one of the buildings and put into a room. There were just six of us; Jankl, Natek, Yacob, Moshe, Berek and myself. We couldn't believe we had a roof over our heads, couldn't believe we would no longer be wet and cold and exposed to the elements. We had a proper mattress to sleep on and the luxury of water coming out of a tap. It was like heaven.

That first night, however, I couldn't sleep as my finger was hurting too much. Next morning I went to the place where the Red Cross was; mostly Swiss, who had taken over Theresienstadt a few days previously. A doctor looked at my finger, gave me an injection, cleaned the wound up and put on a clean dressing for me. After several days I started to feel much better.

However, we were not all so lucky. Maier, my dear friend, who had been shot in the shoulder, died a few days later through lack of medical treatment when on the train. The reason for the long train journey, we found, had been that the Germans were sending us to Theresienstadt to be killed. However, on 8 May, 1945, four days after our arrival, the Russian army liberated us. It was the end of the war in Europe and I had survived!

Russian soldiers are welcomed by prisoners as they
arrive at the gates of Auschwitz main camp in
January 1945. The majority of us, who had been
evacuated away from the advancing Soviets, had to
endure another four months before we could be
liberated.

LIBERATION
8th of May 1945

We knew the German armies were retreating on 7 May, 1945. Many
of the soldiers as they passed Theresienstadt threw in hand grenades
just for the fun of it. That was the day before the liberation and the
end of the war with Germany.

We were all extremely weak and in bad physical condition
from our four weeks' ordeal with that terrible transport from
Buchenwald concentration camp. We all looked alike, our bodies
just skeletons. The six of us who shared the room, Jankl, Natek,
Yacob, Moshe, Berek and myself went to bed that evening utterly
exhausted, but it was not long before I was woken by a commotion
coming from the streets. I heard people shouting and I went to the
window to see what was going on. The sight that met my eyes was
of people trying to climb onto a tank and several jeeps nearby
filled with Russian soldiers, hundreds of people running towards
them. I saw a soldier playing an accordion while others danced.

A DETAIL OF HISTORY

I watched this scene for a few moments, unable to comprehend what was happening; people were actually embracing the soldiers. I thought it was all a dream and shouted to the boys to wake up and come to the window. Slowly the realisation dawned; this was not a dream; it was the moment we had all been praying for. Our joy was indescribable, at that moment I felt I was being born again. We all got dressed as quickly as possible. We just had to go and join the rest of the crowds.

The streets were full of hundreds of people, many of them like us, very weak, hardly able to walk, but wanting to join in this supreme moment of happiness. The smell of free air, being able to walk once again without having a gun in our backs, eating proper food - oh, how I was looking forward to all these things! Maybe some of my family had survived after all, and I would soon be meeting them again. I felt so choked with emotion I could hardly talk.

Natek went off and returned an hour later with his arms laden down with provisions - smoked meat, cheese, butter and chocolate. He told us that the Germans had left a warehouse intact full of food and people were just helping themselves. Imagine how we felt at seeing this kind of food for the first time in five years. To us it was indescribable. We hid the food in our room, putting some of it under our mattresses, not really believing that we would be allowed to keep it. I ate a piece of chocolate, the first in five years; it tasted so, so good. Some of the boys started eating meat, cheese, butter, everything they could lay their hands on and it was not long before they started feeling ill. Their stomachs had been empty for so long, they could not take the rich, fatty foods.

Next morning, 8 May, 1945, I decided that I had to see the defeated German army being rounded up. As weak as I was, I wanted to take revenge for all the suffering they had caused to me,

LIBERATION

my parents, my brother and sisters, all my relatives and all the rest of the Jewish people and the prisoners of war who had not lived to see this day. I asked my friend, Moshe, to accompany me to a town called Leitmeritz that was several kilometres from Theresienstadt. We wanted to watch the columns of German soldiers walking towards the assembly point where they were to be directed to prisoner of war camps. I dragged myself along as best I could to watch this spectacle, to see this invincible army now in defeat. We walked for a while, then managed to hitch a lift from a farmer with a horse and cart who was going our way. Suddenly I spotted them, so we thanked the farmer for his kindness, disembarked and stood on the roadside, watching the rabble of this once so mighty army pass by in twos and threes. A young Russian soldier came over to us with his machine gun and asked us what we wanted. We told him of how we had suffered at the hands of these barbarians. He said he had no love for them either, as the Germans had also committed many atrocities against the Russian people - burning down their villages, plundering their homes and murdering millions.

We told him that we had lost everybody in the war. The roads were now full of Russian soldiers who were smiling at us. 'We are looking at the victors,' we thought.

We stood and watched the defeated *Wehrmacht* army pass. I noticed two SS men and I thought, 'At last my luck has changed.' We told them to stop; one was a sergeant and one a captain. They looked at us in astonishment. The sergeant had a rucksack on his back. "Take it off," I said. He complained that it contained his food and all his belongings. "We have been starved by you for five years," I told him. At that he said he was not a German, but a Frenchman. He had joined the SS, but had never done anything wrong. This was a phrase we were to hear again and again after the war. The captain

A DETAIL OF HISTORY

began to argue with us, his tone arrogant, but he was silenced by the Russian soldier who held up his gun and pointed it at him.

"You Germans are not the masters any more," he said.

We told the SS men that we had only to give the Russian the word and he would shoot both of them. We could see that they were afraid. There was something satisfying about their frightened eyes and trembling bodies. I let them sweat for a moment and then I said, "But we are not murderers like you." We took their food off them and told them to go. We watched as they walked away.

I saw many boys of about my own age in German uniforms, walking towards the assembly camp. At the end of the war the Germans in desperation had been making boys of fifteen into soldiers.

Watching the Germans pass by, it was hard to believe that this dishevelled rabble were the soldiers of whom we had been so terrified. They must have been wondering what the Russians would do to them. Everybody knew how the Germans had treated the Russian people when they invaded Russia. I thought, 'Surely the Germans can't expect any mercy?' I thought of the millions of Jewish people they had tortured and slaughtered and I wondered what punishments would be meted out.

As we watched, a young boy of about my age stopped in front of us, took a knife out of his pocket and silently handed it to me. It was a Hitler Youth knife with a swastika on it. We looked at each other, neither saying a word, then he turned and walked away. Even then that moment seemed poignant to me, and I turned to Moshe and said how happy I was that we had lived to see this day. Clutching the knife and the food we had taken from the SS officers, we made our way back to the camp at Theresienstadt.

The Russians gave us twenty-four hours to do whatever we wanted to the Germans, but being human beings we did nothing.

LIBERATION

On arriving back at Theresienstadt we noticed two cauldrons of rice pudding. I brought out the knife the German boy had handed to me and ate my share of rice pudding ravenously. I thought of my beloved parents, of my dear brother and sisters, and of the many relations and friends who had lost their lives. I prayed for their souls and I prayed for myself.

I wondered then, as I wonder now, whether there was significance in the fact that I had survived. Sometimes I still ask myself whether I was in some way chosen. I kept the German knife for several years, as a souvenir of that terrible war, then somehow, as things do, it got lost.

In any case, such tangible things are not necessary to remind me of the events of 1939 to 1945. It must be left for others to decide whether they had some deep meaning not only for the Jews, but for all mankind, or whether, as the French National Front MP Le Penn said in 1986, my suffering and that of thousands of others was merely a 'detail of history'.

On holiday with my wife Jean in the south of France, in 1983.

POSTSCRIPT

After the war I was taken to England from Theresienstadt (Terezin), Czechoslovakia, with three hundred other children who survived the Holocaust. Originally we were brought to Windermere in the Lake District for recuperation after our ordeal. Here we began to learn English, play games and eat proper food. For the first time since the war we felt human again.

After spending several months there we were split into groups and sent to various cities around the UK. My group was sent to Liverpool, where we stayed in a hostel in Princess Road for eight months before moving on to Manchester in 1947.

Eventually I found my sister, Mania, who survived by escaping into Russia. The rest of my immediate family were murdered by the Nazis. I also found three cousins. One had escaped to Russia, one had come to England in 1939, the third had been through the camps, like me.

A DETAIL OF HISTORY

In 1948 I volunteered to fight in the Israeli Defence Forces to contribute towards the War of Independence. After my fight for survival, I felt it vitally important that there was a homeland for the Jews. I still go there regularly and feel I made a small contribution to its establishment.

I returned to England, married and have three daughters. Today I am retired and live with my wife, Jean, near Leeds. My years have been quiet and happy, as I have lived, worked, and appreciated every moment of the life I now enjoy. For this reason, now that I am retired, I spend some of my time working with young people, sharing my story and reflecting with them on its meaning, past, present and future. I do remember the past. I also think about the future.

Perhaps that, too, is why I wrote this book.

Myself on a return visit to Chelmno in Poland in 1997, the site of the death camp where most of my family were murdered.

Map with pre 1939 borders showing places of Arek Hersh's wartime journey.

The street where we lived in Konin, Poland until 1936.

A street in Sieradz photographed in 1980. The Kloister church can be seen in the background. This was used as an assembly point by the Nazis for the Jews of Sieradz, including my family, before taking and murdering them at Chelmno.

The yard of the Kloister church where I was selected to join a work group. When I left these gates I did not realise I would be separated from my family forever.

The only surviving photograph of family members. These are my cousins posing by a family gravestone in 1935. All my other photographs - the last link I had with my home - were taken from me the day I entered Auschwitz.

Inside the women's block at Birkenau after liberation. This is similar to the barracks I was in. Six people were crammed into each bunk.

Zyklon B. The gas used to murder thousands of people at Birkenau each day.

By the time the Russians liberated us on 8 May 1945, many had died of exposure to the elements and hunger. Their bodies had been removed from the wagons daily. At the start of the evacuation, there had been 100 prisoners in this wagon. Most died.

Two months after liberation we had put on weight again. I am on the far left of the picture. All of us had lost our families and were cared for in the Theresienstadt camp.

The Boys and Girls, all orphans and survivors of the catastrophe which decimated the Jewish communities of Europe. Pictured here in Prague, August 1945, just three months after liberation and a few days before our departure for England. I am second on the left in the second row.

Our group of 300, mostly boys, were flown to England in Lancaster bombers and taken to Windermere on 14 August 1945. Here some of us have an English lesson. I am in the second row, fourth from the right.

My sister Mania in 1947.
She was the only other
surviving member of my
immediate family. She had
been taken to Soviet
occupied territory by my
auntie as the Germans
invaded Poland.

I went to Israel and fought
in the War of Independence
in 1948. Later I returned to
England where I settled and
had three children. Pictured
here in 1980.